THE PILLARS OF SOCIETY

The Pillars

of Society

SIX CENTURIES OF CIVILIZATION IN THE NETHERLANDS

by

WILLIAM Z. SHETTER

MARTINUS NIJHOFF / THE HAGUE / 1971

ISBN 90 247 5080 6

Contents

An introductory word

A recent book analyzing the contemporary political structure in the Netherlands calls the key chapter 'The rules of the game'. Another one, written in the Netherlands a few years ago and attempting to give a picture of some of the most characteristic features of the country's social organization, symbolizes its essence with a cartoon about card games. A world-famous historian derives an entire book about the play-element in culture from the culture of the late Medieval Netherlands.

In trying to account to myself for the unity of the culture of the Netherlands over a wide range of phenomena and through many centuries of history, I found myself toying with the thought that the elusive but characteristic flavor of the culture might be approached by means of the currently fashionable idea of a game. With proper restraint, it ought to be possible to explain some fundamental things about the culture by means of a small number of quite simple rules, the sort of habits and tendencies that are not always easy for an insider to notice but that are obvious enough once pointed out by someone who has had to learn them. Ideally such rules ought to be the kind about which it can be shown that cultural history is a large, panoramic playing out of them and that conspicuous creations like art and literature are in some sense manifestations of them. Past achievements and present pattern ought to be inseparable from each other.

It is this kind of a presentation of the culture of the Netherlands that is being undertaken in the pages to follow. There are no startling new

1

insights into historical events nor radical reinterpretations of art or literature, but rather a running commentary on present and past that singles out what seem to me to be the deeply rooted themes that constantly generate the events and works we see up on the surface. The most radical departure from any other treatment of the history and structure of the culture is probably the close attention given to the language itself. Having always felt a vague dissatisfaction at the way the language is seldom treated as if it had much relation to the development of political systems or the creation of artistic phenomena, I resolved that if I ever had occasion to present the culture as a totality I would correct this by attempting to show that the language is probably the prime exponent of the rules being followed by the culture. Though social dimensions in the way the language is used are going to be of central importance, I should hasten to add that I assume no control of the language on the part of readers. All Dutch quotations will be found in English at the bottom of the page, and all translations, incidentally, are my own.

The chapters to follow, then, are an attempt by an outside observer to explain something of the nature of the culture of the Netherlands to other outsiders. The number of these chapters readily betrays its origin in the academic semester, and I cheerfully acknowledge the stimulating discussions with students without which this would probably not have taken concrete shape. However, it is not intended primarily as a textbook but more generally as an exercise, for anyone interested, in a type of cross-cultural understanding. Large numbers of members of my own culture have close contact with that of the Netherlands, and it can only be called unfortunate that the modern, industrialized face worn by the Netherlands today effectively masks the striking uniqueness of the cultural patterns under the surface that continue to provide the country with its own style in the European context. It was attempts to explain these underlying cultural patterns, first to myself and later to others, that gradually led me to perceive that social patterns, the using of the language, and the achievements of the past were all part of the same fundamental rules.

Some serious-minded readers will no doubt object to the overly light-hearted way in which the 'game' idea tends to be applied to very weighty and complex matters. My only answer would be that a degree of irresponsibility is always a hazard in a brief presentation of a large subject, and that I trust the attentive reader will sense where a grain of salt is appropriate. A more serious objection, and a legitimate one, will be that the picture here is too selective, never even mentioning many important persons and events, and worse, that it has a habit of treating the culture as if it always existed in isolation. The best answer to this is to disclaim any pretense of offering a complete work on cultural history and to point out that understanding of the total cultural picture will be greatly enhanced by some additional reading. In fact, the publisher's concurrence with my wish that the cost of this sketch be kept as low as possible means that in the absence of the illustrations and maps that it would have been good to include, the reader will find it necessary to have an illustrated cultural history at his elbow as he reads. The histories to which I am most indebted and the cultural histories that will be most useful to the reader are listed at the beginning of the Notes, which are to be found immediately following Chapter 15.[1]

While I was still in my teens, I once began corresponding with a young lady my own age in the Netherlands, and soon after this found myself buying a little do-it-yourself grammar of Dutch to see if I could manage to compose an intelligible sentence or two. At that time I would no doubt have been astonished if someone had predicted that over twenty years later I would have gotten to know the country well and developed an increasing fascination with its people and its history. This 'outsider's view' will seem to many of them to be a bit idiosyncratic here and there, but I would like to think it offers a perspective that is just different enough to be interesting without being wrong-headed. It is offered as an attempt to repay my debt to the many people who enriched my experience – often without realizing they were doing it – by patiently helping me during these years to learn the language and understand something about the culture, and I hope it will be accepted in this spirit.

April, 1970

3

1 *The pillars of society*

Since it is only reasonable to expect a title to give fair indication of what is to come, we ought to start by making sure our general title awakens all the right associations. To most speakers of English, the word 'pillars' in this context probably suggests first of all important people, in Dutch cultural history perhaps people such as Erasmus, William the Silent and some of the great 17th-century commercial and political leaders. To some it might also suggest the basic institutions that hold a society together, such as democratic government or religion, or perhaps even more abstract things such as peacefulness, decency and tolerance.

If the title conjures up these images, it has done at least part of its job right. We are about to start considering precisely this kind of highlights as we follow a varied and colorful civilization through the most important and interesting periods of its history. The Netherlands is the most densely populated country in Europe, and is situated in a strategic corner of the continent where for many centuries it has been exposed to an intensive traffic in goods and ideas. Not only is the land itself derived from other places, as a Dutch historian pointed out – it consists largely of sand and clay washed down by the large rivers that cross it and laid down on a foundation brought by glaciers in the Ice Age – but nearly all the cultural advances we immediately think of in connection with the Netherlands were really borrowed from elsewhere. The Burgundian courtly culture came from France, late Medieval painting from Italy, Calvinism from Switzerland, Renaissance poetry from Italy, and even the 17th-century painters, probably the most distinctively Dutch of them all, did not develop their technique from nowhere but got much of it from the Italians.

To say all this, though, is of course to say nothing very significant, since such cultural manifestations are always the results of a slow development and a borrowing back and forth across borders. What is significant is the particular synthesis made by one people of a constant cultural bombardment from without – how it shaped its borrowings to its own particular needs and made them into a uniquely individual expression of itself. Much of what we feel to be important Dutch contributions to our Western civilization – painting perhaps first and foremost, but equally important the development of exacting observation in science, the evolution of a novel, republican, form of the state, contributions to international law and to education and trade – is well enough known that its importance hardly needs to be defended here. Quite the contrary, it has become so familiar that there is a considerable danger of our accepting these surface manifestations of a culture without troubling to ask the question how it came about. Surely achivements such as these can only be the products of a viable, well-functioning society, a people responding to the complex challenges of an environment (whether these be physical, economic, military or some other) by creating a culture that provides each member with an image of the whole he is a part of. We will return in a moment to the idea of culture and consider just how we are to understand the term.

If we want to be more than merely casual observers, then, we will want to know what kind of a people it was that found its expression and its image in what we call the civilization of the Netherlands, and – to the extent that we can – why it responded the way it did to the particular pressures and challenges imposed on it. We will see in due course that the period in which this culture reached its fullest development lasted almost precisely a century: from 1555, the date of the accession of Philip II to the Spanish throne, the fatal event that soon

5

led to the revolt of the Netherlands, to 1648, the date of the Treaty of Westphalia that ended the Thirty Years' War and established the independence of the Dutch Republic. It is in this climax period, the culmination of several centuries of development that set the tone of all subsequent history and gave the culture of the Netherlands the stamp it still bears, that we will want to ask who and what the 'pillars' were; which persons were most responsible for the development of an integrated and cohesive society; which cultural institutions are the key ones that give us insight into the direction developments are taking. To ask these questions intelligently we ought to make sure we have some understanding of the contemporary culture of the Netherlands that is the direct heir to this past. And this brings us back once more to our title.

Since we are about to undertake an exercise in cross-cultural under-standing, it seemed excusable to allow the title to contain a pun which requires for appreciation of it certain very important information about modern Dutch society. The play is on the same word 'pillars', which in Dutch is *zuilen*, a word with a similar architectural meaning but a vastly different sociological one. The 'pillars' of society in the Dutch sense are social arrangements that can justly be called a purely Dutch invention, since sociologists seem to be in agreement that there is no reasonably exact parallel to be found in any other modern society.[1] *Zuilen,* in a word, are the confessional-political blocs into which modern Dutch society is divided and which thoroughly perme-ate nearly every aspect of contemporary life in the Netherlands. Their number varies depending on the observer and how he chooses to define them; they are very complex and resist easy definition, but they are so important to an understanding of life in the Netherlands that most of Chapter 2 will be devoted to an attempt to explain their function. At this point we need not go any farther than a remark or two about their relation to the past, to the civilization of the Netherlands as it developed especially in our century-long period on both sides of the year 1600. In the present-day Netherlands we have a society thoroughly split up into a small set of groups such that a person by virtue of his religious, political and other preferences 'belongs' in one and therefore automatically not in any other, the result of which is that the invisible lines existing in any society between 'us' and 'them' tend to be unusually sharply drawn. Lest this social system seem unduly ferocious, however, the reverse side of the coin must be shown as well: This split into groups is accepted by most members of the society as perfectly natural, and indeed some are quite unaware that other societies are based on a rather different structure. In principle the *zuilen* are thought of as coordinate and equal, the separate but inviolable 'pillars' on which – to return to the architectural sense – society rests. The chasms betweem them are bridged over by a highly-developed feeling for the necessity of respect for another's views, no matter how strongly one may be opposed to them; if the sanctity of his belief is threatened, one's own is equally vulnerable. It should be obvious by this point that a society formed from a number of distinct groups can only function if its members have had long, hard practice in the difficult art of toleration. It is this 'long, hard practice' that gives us our link with the history of Dutch civilization.

Is the concept and application of religious toleration something that it was the destiny of a particularly enlightened people to evolve? The Dutch are often given credit for developing a very modern form of religious and political toleration at a time when the rest of the world seemed the very opposite of gentle and accepting. This is not a question that can be answered with yes or no, but one thing our excursion into history will show us is that for the ancestors of the people of the present-day Netherlands toleration was not a luxury of civilization but a matter of brute necessity on the one hand and a practical matter of good business on the other. We hope to see, as we go along, how the circumstances of history tend to encourage the formation of a specific social structure. But history is not blind chance: an already-existing tendency toward a certain style of inter-action turned and formed historical events, transformed a potential disaster into a cultural flowering and impressed a unique form on this culture. This last statement simply means that as we begin considering the gradual development of something we can eventually identify as a specifically Dutch type of ·culture, we should deliberately use whatever social guideposts the present provides and look for how much of this 'style of interaction' can be tracked down.

The divisive effect of the splitting of Dutch society into separate *zuilen* can easily be overdramatized. As a matter of fact most foreign observers are struck by a remarkable, at times downright monotonous, homogeneity in Dutch life, a fact pointed out over and over by Goudsblom in the book mentioned above. With due allowance made for the very real differences that exist depending on religion, politics, social level and geographical area, there can be no question that there is a very highly-developed, almost 'monolithic' Dutch culture participated in by all members of the society, and readily distinguishable from all others, for instance those of its neighbors Belgium, France, Germany and England. The most ready symbol of this standardization – though only in a restricted sense its cause – is the existence of a standard cultural language that overlies the multitude of local dialects that merge in the east with those of Germany; its development, which we will return to a few chapters farther on, is completely bound up with the social developments of the crucial period that brought about the very homogeneity of culture we are talking about. Going somewhat deeper than the language – which has the additional limitation that the same standard language is used by the distinctly different culture of the northern half of Belgium – we can observe that modern Dutch culture tends strongly to foster a certain definite set of outlooks, aspirations and moral standards that show very little variance attributable to one's position in the social structure. In other words, people of all kinds tend to think in similar ways about things, and it is probably not too bold an oversimplification to say that there exists a characteristically Dutch personality type. While the culture places considerable weight, as we just saw, on the avoidance of direct challenge to another's position to the extent that this position represents his innermost guiding beliefs, we will presently have occasion to see that at the same time it attaches notable importance to a certain outward conformity to an overall standard of behavior. The culture tends to mold the personalities of its members in two distinct but very closely related ways: one who grows up within it is taught to accept (though not necessarily to admire) basic beliefs that are radically different, and at the same time to be very conscious of deviations from the set of standards held to be binding on all members of the culture. Languages have a way of displaying in the elaborate specialization of certain areas of their stock of words what is of particular importance to their underlying cultures; in Chapter 14 we will illustrate briefly the means that members of Dutch culture use for talking about these 'binding standards'.

Although both the words 'society' and 'civilization' are used in the title, the word 'culture' has occurred even more often in our discussion so far and shows, if anything, even more signs of being a key term. Since in fact all three of these words are important to our thinking about the past and the present in the Netherlands, we might well pause a moment to consider what each of them implies.

'Society' is the most general of the three. It simply means any kind of banding together into some kind of organization, however rudimentary, for mutual benefit. Man forms societies, but many animals show social behavior as well. But whereas animals follow a rigid instinctual pattern, human social behavior is only partly instinctive and appears in a great variety of forms that are imposed on it by something else we call culture. When we speak of Dutch society, we mean whatever has to do with this 'banding together' itself, particularly the more concrete organizational aspect that affects the everyday lives of people in practical ways and serves to interweave people's lives with each other. Society is usually thought of as continuous; in the case of Dutch society we might say that it extends up to the national borders, thus covering the entire area that is under the authority of the central government. The word 'society' in the title is meant to imply that its 'pillars' – in both the English and the Dutch senses – are very

9

practical things, whether they may be people, principles or items in the social structure itself, that help to hold a large group of people together in a harmonious type of interaction.

Whereas 'society' can be applied to ants and bees just as well as to mankind, the word 'culture' clearly separates man off from all other species. It is probably most simply defined as the sum total of all learned behavior that is shared by all members of a society. Here the important word 'learned' signals that the behavior in question is not a result of instinct but depends on memory, which in turn is thoroughly bound up with man's apparently unique ability to free himself from his immediate environment and reflect. Above all, culture depends on the possession of a language as a means of symbolizing, storing and passing on gains. Culture, unlike instinct, is cumulative.

By 'culture', then, we will mean a type of patterned behavior that goes beyond – usually quite far beyond – the rudiments of social organization that would probably suffice for mere survival. Even the most materially primitive culture known does not stop at the stage of social aggregation but provides, by means of a highly complex symbolic system, an integrated and complete structuring of the world for its members. Society gives the individual safety and some means for assuring the basic necessities for survival, but culture (which includes this as well, thus overlapping with the idea of 'society') contributes the whole vast abstract side that only humans find necessary because it is a direct consequence of our ability to reflect: it makes meaningful and intelligible to the members of a society the great mysteries of one's self, relations between people, and the whole intangible realm beyond the observable. It does this by finding in man something larger than himself, in other words by creating religion. It is therefore not unreasonable to say that the whole phenomenon of culture, without which man would scarcely be distinguishable from other animal species, resides in the gap between man and nature that results from his act of stepping back and seeing himself separate from it, and by means of its almost infinite variety of religious ritual strives to bridge this gap by making nature's mysteries intelligible.

The most important aspect of culture is that in providing an accounting for 'the way things are' it gives each individual a meaningful image of his own place in the total picture. Primitive cultures illustrate all this more easily than complex modern Western ones, but we have just seen a fairly clear example of how Dutch culture tends to shape and nurture the personalities of its members in certain set ways by laying down standards of behavior to which the individual is expected to adhere. Culture consists of a channeling of behavior, a set of constraints which the members of a culture normally regard not at all as arbitrary but, on the contrary, as sacred and immutable. Such constraints on behavior have the very practical function of making a multitude of minute decisions unnecessary and leaving the individual free to act in those areas where the culture allows choice. In spite of the great variety of ways in which cultures set the pattern of hopes, fears and aspirations for their members, the constraints are not felt to be such — in fact, usually they are not felt at all. Even in moving between two cultures as similar in many ways as the Dutch and the American, members on both sides are inevitably struck by attitudes and styles of social interaction that can seem, at their worst, perverse and unreasonable.

Culture is an elaborate set of rules imposed on a basic physical and social reality, a complex of understandings shared in by a limited group of people following these rules (though, as we just said, usually unaware that they are) who — at least in the modern world — are conscious of the existence of those not participating; in other words, there are insiders and outsiders. At this point, the similarity to what we commonly define as a 'game' is too obvious to be passed by. What we actually seem to be saying is that culture is like a great game, played by a definable group according to definable rules, something that is clearly set off from ordinary, physical reality. The fact that culture is perfectly serious does not, it should be noted, prevent it from containing a strong strain of the 'make-believe'. Though there are reasons for being rather hesitant about calling every culture a 'game', we will see in our fourth chapter that this idea works surprisingly well in providing some illumination about the culture of the Netherlands, and it is surely no accident that it was a member of this same culture, the historian Huizinga, who conceived the idea of treating culture as the essence of 'play' or a 'game'. The title of *Homo ludens* 'man the player'[2] shows his view of the essential distinguishing feature of man, the culture-builder, and his *Herfsttij der middeleeuwen*,[3] known in English as *The waning of the Middle Ages*, is the analysis of the Medieval culture of the area including the Netherlands that inspired the idea in the first place. Let us experiment with thinking about Dutch culture of whatever period in somewhat this sort of way: as a set of traditional rules for behavior and for the interpretation of life that are generally accepted by the participants, taught to children, and so passed on through the generations, changing only imperceptibly until a sufficient historical perspective is gained. We have already seen two rules of this earnest game in its contemporary form: tolerate different fundamental beliefs, but be less tolerant of deviations from universal standards of social behavior. In going back into the past, our task will now be to try to discover, after we have spent Chapter 2 outlining more rules of the 'game' in its modern form, what some of the rules were that made sense to people in the past and that might account for the outer manifestations of culture we read about in all our texts. What 'game' — and it was a deadly serious one — was being played in the late 1500's and early 1600's when the history of Dutch culture reached its peak?

Up to this point we have talked about only the intangible, non-material aspect of culture, the abstract principles that give form to belief and therefore lie at its heart. Since these arise from the social experience of an interacting group, we are justified in restricting our view to the culture of a single society — however fluid its boundaries have been in the past. Still, it is too tempting to forget that this culture is after all no more than a permutation of general Western culture and that its system of beliefs, however distinctly Dutch, is part

12

of the dominant institution of Western culture that we call Christianity. This distinctness within a larger framework is most obvious in the realm of material culture, the artifacts that every culture produces as an expression of its non-material side. While we are scrutinizing Dutch architecture, painting and literature for what we can learn about their connections to the underlying 'game', we hope to remain aware of the vigorous give-and-take among the various European cultures. We can readily see here what is also true of the non-material realm: The Netherlands absorbed cultural gains from neighboring societies but transformed them into unique forms of expression of itself, and then — in its best-integrated, harmonious periods — gave them back to the other participants in Western culture in greatly enriched form.

We began with the idea of 'society' and moved from there to 'culture'. In concentrating our interest on the culture of the Netherlands with its highly-developed material and non-material response to the environment, we have ended up talking about what usually goes by the less technical name of 'civilization'. If we were studying an isolated culture in the highlands of New Guinea we would have no need of this term, but in the case of Dutch culture, as in the case of any European culture, it suggested itself in the title more readily than did the really key term 'culture'. The reason for this is not only that 'civilization' is a more popular and readily suggestive word than 'culture', but because it carries with it a useful reminder that the culture of the Netherlands is really a sub-culture participating in Western civilization. 'Civilization' as it is popularly used implies a high level of technological achievement, an enlightened exploitation of human resources, and the development of writing, arts and sciences, cities and statecraft. A civilization is generally thought of as a particularly long-lived and widely-diffused form of culture; there are probably thousands of distinct cultures in the world, but there are and have been only a few civilizations. Our talking about 'civilization' in the Netherlands is meant to imply, then, that we will be concerned with many of these highly complex and advanced manifestations of culture.

13

To sum up: The Netherlands represents for us a SOCIETY, composed of people interacting on the practical level, at the same time a CIVILIZATION participating in a highly sophisticated larger one that offered the society the means to give expression to itself, but most fundamentally a CULTURE, a set of uniquely Dutch ways of playing a serious and fascinating game.

2 Some rules of the game

On January 4, 1964, a Saturday evening, millions of television viewers in the Netherlands watched a program called *Zo is het toevallig ook nog 's een keer,* a half-hour satirical show on current events that was modeled on the then popular BBC show called This was the week that was, and that had come to be known simply as *Zo is het* 'that's the way it is'. This particular program, the third in the series, contained a scene in which one of the actors was shown dressed as a minister. He reminded viewers of the ministers who appear regularly in religious programs on TV, except that he proceeded to satirize the 'worship' of TV itself in a mock sermon that rephrased passages from Genesis, the Ten Commandments and the New Testament in addition to making a play on the word *zending* 'mission' instead of *uitzending* 'broadcast'. The scene showed TV antennas when the word 'cross' was mentioned, and ended with the following words:

En zo won dit machtige geloof elke dag nieuwe discipelen die gelijk met hun broeders en zusters neerknielen voor het Beeld en bidden: Geef ons heden ons dagelijks programma, wees met ons, o Beeld, want wij weten niet wat wij zonder u zouden moeten doen.*

Certainly a good bit of this was in somewhat poor taste, and in the

* And so every day this mighty faith gained new disciples, who with their brothers and sisters kneel before the Picture and pray: Give us this day our daily program. Abide with us, o Picture, for we know not what we would do without thee.

U.S. would undoubtedly have provoked some protests from individuals who had felt offended by it, perhaps also from religious groups resenting its disrespect toward matters sacred to some people. In the Netherlands, the result was an absolutely unparalleled storm of controversy that convulsed the country from the Cabinet on down and for the whole following week crowded virtually everything else from the newspapers and engulfed Letters to the Editor columns. Weeks later the whole affair was still being vigorously debated in the public press; within the month a paperback book appeared entitled simply *Zo is het,*[1] which presented some early reactions and analyses, those 'for' the program on the left-hand page and those 'against' on the right — an arrangement with an obvious political import. In 1966, after two years of cooling off and reflection had elapsed, another paperback appeared: *Beeldreligie,*[2] a critical analysis of the whole phenomenon written by two professional observers, a political scientist and a historian. Many prominent citizens have in the meantime and since then offered an interpretation in interviews and in writing, and most of the well-known literary figures have by now had something to say about this peculiarly Dutch phenomenon. This last phrase is used quite deliberately. It seems that nothing of this amazing turmoil ever found its way into the press in this country, not because the Netherlands is small and unimportant — matters pertaining to the Royal Family are regularly reported in detail — but undoubtedly because it would have been nearly impossible to explain to a public unfamiliar with Dutch society just what it was all about.

When a social disruption of this magnitude is triggered by an example of bad taste that is perhaps blatant but surely not by itself of national scope, it suggests strongly that there is much more to it than appears on the surface, that the offensive lapse of taste itself is only a symptom. To be even more specific, the convulsive reaction of the whole society suggests that a balance was upset, that a very important 'rule of the game' was somehow broken. Often we find ourselves in the best position to discover the inner workings of a system when it goes wrong or breaks down, so accordingly we might exploit this very obvious disruption to try to find out what important cultural factors are at work here.

By the middle of the week immediately following that Saturday evening one thing became evident that has been pointed out by numerous observers since then: much of the flood of abusive, often anomymous protest (the 'right' as defined by the *Zo is het* paperback) had little to do with the program itself – large numbers of threats and insults were directed against an actress who had appeared on the program but who had had no connection with the TV satire itself[3] – appeared to be pent-up resentment for which an outlet had finally presented itself. But this is not yet the heart of the matter. A closer look at the articles and letters that appeared in the newspaper in those first days shows that many Dutch citizens, mainly those on the 'left', but also some on the 'right', were accusing each other of hyprocrisy, saying in effect 'Are the religious symbols really all that sacred to you, or are you offended only because of who it was that misused them? ' Looking still further, we find that indeed significant numbers of the letters and articles contain a tone of political polemic that would seem entirely out of place in a protest one of us might express about an instance of poor taste on a TV program. A satire of the sort we are talking about presented by one of our large networks would certainly have called forth some protest, but it would probably not occur to any of those who felt offended that the network had any sinister political motives, nor would any host of fellow citizens rise up to accuse those offended of being motivated by something quite removed from sincere religious convictions. This is because the networks are national institutions lacking identification with the persuasions of any particular segment of the society. Many of the Dutch protesters, however, made direct and indirect reference to the fact that this TV program was produced by an organization identified with the Socialist political bloc, and concluded that a large segment of the population commonly thought of – not always very accurately – as being 'against' religion or at least indifferent to it had launched a deliberate attack on those segments of the population to whom

17

religion was important – even if, as some letters seem to suggest, its function is little more than providing a badge of anti-Socialism, a conclusion unhesitatingly drawn by many on the 'left'. What happened, then, is that the organization responsible for the program was not national at all but the arm of one social group, and its action in presenting a satire was widely interpreted as an offense not against religion itself but against other social groups it should have respected. These are, of course, the *zuilen* we have already mentioned, the composition of which is one of the central facts about the Dutch way of life.

Starting with the outermost organizational aspects of this unique phenomenon, we might say the society consists of a set of coordinate groups with solidarity toward the inside and separation toward the outside. This is, on the surface, nothing but the 'in-group' and 'out-group' system that can be found in every society, but in the Netherlands it has reached proportions found nowhere else in a society that nevertheless manages to function as a harmonious whole. These coordinate groups are defined by sociologists as integrated complexes of social organizations – and thus not merely one single set of social organizations – on the basis of an ultimate guiding persuasion, neatly indicated in Dutch by the untranslatable word *levensbeschouwing*. These are called *zuilen*, a word that does not seem to have taken on this meaning until after the second World War, and the whole phenomenon itself is referred to as *verzuiling;* particularly this latter word carries for many people a connotation of condemnation, though there is no other accepted technical term for the social reality involved.

To do justice to an extremely complex phenomenon would take a great many pages here; two sketches of the nature of *verzuiling* for Dutch readers are offered by Kruijt[4], who has come to be probably the foremost specialist on it, and a very intelligible explanation of it in English is given by Goudsblom[5]. The two largest and most inclusive *zuilen* are the Roman Catholic one and the orthodox Protestant one. This is true, as we will see later on, for perfectly good historical reasons, inasmuch as these represent the two large underprivileged segments of the population that in the last century took up a fight for equal recognition and for support for separate schools. The meaning of the phrase 'integrated complex of social organizations' is that each of these groups includes church, political conviction, schools, newspapers and radio and TV outlets, charity organizations, hospitals and leisure-time groups. In other words, a person who belongs to a given church will normally vote a certain way, send his children to a certain school, subscribe to a certain newspaper, support a certain radio and TV corporation, and so on. Though of course a person is perfectly free to vote one way and to read an entirely different type of newspaper, the statistics that show approximately equal numbers of people belonging to a given church, voting a given way, supporting a given TV corporation and subscribing to a given newspaper suggest a high degree of conformity to one's own *zuil*. People do in fact seem to function largely within a certain bloc where a whole range of social patterns are relatively predictable. With certain reservations, it is not exaggerating to claim that picking up a TV guide in someone's home (each TV corporation publishes its own and broadcasting time is allotted according to number of subscribers) enables one to say the general direction in which his religious preference lies, which party he votes for, and which daily paper is dropped through the mail slot in the evening.

The crucial point, however, is not just that such inclusive-exclusive organizations exist, but that the entire society is composed of them, implying that merely being a member of Dutch society involves belonging to one *zuil* or another. Besides the two largest there are two smaller ones, those of the liberal Protestants and the Humanists, which have probably arisen for largely defensive reasons as counterbalances to the exclusiveness of the two large ones. The fifth bloc, comparable in size to the two largest, is the Socialist one. Some sociologists claim that it is not a *zuil* at all because it is not organized around any *levensbeschouwing*, but we do not need to be this puristic, since the Dutch public certainly does regard is as one. This absence of

19

a philosophical commitment other than a political one, though, is precisely what makes the 'red' *zuil* especially interesting to us and in fact contains the key to our problem. The modern Socialist group tries consciously to separate religion and politics by achieving a 'breakthrough' in the Dutch social system where people of all persuasions can find a political and social home. A person would then not have to be labeled either confessional or neutral with no other choice, but his religious outlook would simply be irrelevant to his politics – a self-evident idea to us, but one that runs counter to a very old tradition in Dutch life. If we now look back one more time to our TV show with the knowledge that it was broadcast by the Socialist *zuil*, the strong reaction to a real or fancied offense shows that a large part of Dutch society is extraordinarily sensitive to any upsetting of the natural and accepted balance of the various *zuilen*, particularly in the case of a *zuil* with a history of a certain degree of antagonism. The real underlying significance of a social disturbance in the Netherlands can in fact often be gauged by the number of political cartoons that display Greek columns.

The *verzuiling* system is firmly established, and there is no sign that Dutch society is moving toward a different form of social organization. Quite the contrary, many feel that the system is becoming steadily more entrenched in the Dutch way of life. Though the *zuilen* as they exist today are hardly older than the present century, they are nothing revolutionary at all but simply a modern form of certain very old and well-established aspects of social life in the Netherlands, a logical outward manifestation of a social organization that has changed relatively little in the last three and a half centuries. Members of all societies are alike in feeling the institutions developed by their culture to be natural and appropriate frameworks for all types of human interaction. Even though *verzuiling* is itself a frequent object of satire and its pros and cons are endlessly debated, every conceivable kind of social shortcoming having been blamed on it at one time or another, the average individual finds that the social structure he inherited gives him a context for meaningful and self-fulfilling relationships with other members of his society. Since we have just finished outlining a rather awesome system of mutually walled-off blocs within a single one of which the individual's social life tends to move, how this could lead to anything but fragmentation and mutual suspicion might require a few words of explanation.

Dutch society makes its own compensation for the pluralism characteristic of *verzuiling* in a highly-developed social standard of propriety which places a conspicuous value on a general mutual respect. The specific formalization of this that is entered into by all members of the society and that makes possible smooth social relations through the walls of *verzuiling* might best be termed simply a polite reserve. 'Polite' because the individual is expected to use a number of traditional formulas of greeting, address and conversation which develop a certain easy cordiality while at the same time leaving scrupulously untouched the other person's private business; thus everyday social interaction proceeds on a level of mutual respect that never touches one's identification with a particular *zuil,* though it would be irresponsible not to go on to point out that the Dutch are extremely skilled at the art of picking up little signals − such as the TV guide mentioned above − that make this identification readily known, resulting in a certain discrepancy between what is understood and what is actually said. Another very important value attached to this exercise of polite respect for others, with all its employment of obligatory niceties of word, gesture and custom, is the prestige that reflects back on the user himself. The individual is taught to be conscious that in observing proper politeness and in maintaining an appropriate control of the standard language he is demonstrating himself to be a full-fledged member of polite society who knows 'how things should be done' and is therefore elegible for precisely the same respect in return. This concern for one's own social image is frequently denounced in emotional terms as a type of national neurosis, but as a means of integrating the individual into general social life it is an important ingredient in contemporary Dutch life.

'Reserve', the other main component of the phrase 'polite reserve', is the social requirement that the other person be held at a certain distance. This has already made itself evident in the rule which forbids prying into another's personal convictions or even betraying that one knows anything about them ... at least until the relationship has developed to a more intimate level. Demonstrating that one knows 'how things should be done' also involves giving evidence of a proper rein on the emotions, in general not acting in any way that will call undue attention to oneself. A newcomer in a neighborhood or a social group is normally left alone until he chooses to introduce himself; though his presence is known, to attempt to bring him into the group would be an embarrassing invasion of his right to solitude — a right highly prized in a densely populated country. It is easy to see by now how an outsider from another culture, even a closely related one, often finds himself confronted with a bewildering complex of invisible walls that he finds it difficult to make sense of. But the 'rules of the game' here are nothing more than the Dutch adaptation of common European middle-class ideals that value an outer politeness together with a strong interest in the doings of one's neighbors.

The general diffusion in European cultures of an interplay between the intimate and the polite is probably nowhere more plainly visible than in the forms of address to which it has given rise in the modern standard languages. The same distinction between familiar and polite words for 'you' is found everywhere — having been lost again only in English — but its exact social distribution is different in each case. The Dutch standard language uses the pronoun *u* as an indicator that the polite type of social relationship is being observed. In general one uses this in addressing all those toward whom one is moving on a level of respectful distance, those who are equal members of society but with whom one is engaged (at least for the time being) in a relationship on a single level only, for instance a professional or commercial one. By showing respect and distance, one deserves and expects the same in return, a perfect symbolization of an important rule in the game. The type of social solidarity that exists on the familiar level is signaled by the use of *jij*. This is used with all those toward whom one does not have to create a respectful distance, for the relationships which by virtue of birth and relation or by virtue of mutual understanding permit intrusion into the personal areas of first name, casual style of speaking, one's *levensbeschouwing* and the like – in short, the relationships in which one is not (or at least not so obviously) in the position of being subjected to social judgement. Social interaction being as complex as it is, however, things are often not this simple. There are many cases in which one might not return the 'respectful distance' of *u*, for instance toward someone not considered a member of the society of equals such as someone under about 15 or – as an infrequent relic of a bygone era – a social inferior; or, if one is old enough, toward a person a generation or so younger with whom one chooses to adopt a somewhat paternal role. But these complexities, along with the numerous kinds of embarrassing doubt that can arise when one is not sure enough of one's relationship to a person to be able to decide in a given situation which form of address is appropriate, only serve to underline the social importance of the two very different kinds of solidarity involved: the complex intimate one that is full of personal implications and the relatively unidimensional world-at-large one behind which one retreats. Still, it is the latter that is more interesting to us here. *Jij* is everybody's family heritage, but it is *u* that first reaches over from one *zuil* to the other and so gives constant assurance of the rules that hold everything together.

Probably the chief instrument of homogeneity is the standard language itself, which in Dutch is commonly known as *algemeen beschaafd*, implying that this form of the language is the same for everyone and that it serves as an accepted vehicle of the culture. Over the centuries a generally western form of speech has come into common use throughout the country, bringing with it, as did the standard language in every European country, the dominant nation-wide cultural standards and weakening – though in most cases not obliterating – the hold of local dialect and local ways. The role played in this process by schools, later by radio and now by TV is very little different from the one we find elsewhere, but the nature of the social pressures behind acceptance of the standard cultural language are perhaps unique to the Netherlands. We noted in passing earlier in this chapter that a person's valued social prestige comes at least partly from his evidencing proper control of the standard language as a mark of his control of the 'proper' forms of the culture itself. His use of the language is thus an easily perceptible badge of his eligibility to be treated as a full equal. It is not as if he would be patronized with *jij* without it – at least not today any longer – but it remains a fact that speaking a substandard form of the language will forever stand in the way of his rising economically beyond a certain level. Though dialect or even strongly dialect-flavored speech erects a social barrier of which everyone is aware, a certain degree of accent left by one's place of origin is almost unavoidable and indeed worn proudly by some; it is part of the characteristic Dutch interest in their neighbors that they enjoy their often remarkably accurate ability to place each other geographically.

Besides serving to transmit cultural ideals, there are other ways in which a language gives direct expression to social facts that are important to the culture it serves. All of them, for instance, show some type of differentiation of stylistic levels reflecting the various types of social situation that may come about in their own particular culture. In the Netherlands as everywhere else, people speak casually and carelessly in some situations while in others they pay somewhat more attention to pronunciation, grammar and choice of words. It is tempting to call one, somewhat tongue in cheek, a kind of *jij*-style and the other a more *u*-style, though in actuality there are probably a number of finely-graded stylistic levels matching the various degrees of casualness or formality a speaker may feel.

But there exists a much more striking stylistic opposition that is a peculiarly well-adapted expression of Dutch culture, one that is found in some other speech communities but that is not universal. Anyone who gains control of the everyday spoken language, whether he learns

24

it as a Dutch child at home or as an adult foreigner, is sooner or later faced with the necessity, if he is to participate fully in the workings of Dutch society, of learning another style which is rather sharply distinct from the group of closely similar spoken styles. He must assimilate a new vocabulary, the basic nature of which is illustrated by *reeds* for the colloquial *al* 'already', *thans* for *nu* 'now', *daar* for *omdat* 'because', *geheel* for *helemaal* 'entirely', *gereed* for *klaar* 'ready', and even *rijwiel* for *fiets* 'bicycle'. Though the difference is largely a matter of vocabulary, he must also control a number of syntactic devices he would not use in speaking – a probably inevitable consequence of the evolution of a literary language. One striking example of this is the use of the feminine gender in association with historically feminine nouns and the use of the genitive case, both of which have long since vanished from common colloquial use. This usage has developed a step further in relatively recent times into a particularly interesting example of the social exploitation of an orig-inally purely grammatical fact. The feminine gender, especially in the form of the pronoun *zij* 'she, it', *haar* 'her, their, its', and the genitive form of the article *der,* has become so completely identified in the feeling of many speakers with literary elegance rather than grammat-ical function that these forms are now frequently used in connection with masculine and even neuter nouns . . . with predictable reactions from the camp of the grammatical purists.[6]

The Dutch call these two styles spoken language and written language, *spreektaal* and *schrijftaal,* because in the simplest terms one tends to speak in one fashion but to cultivate a separate, artificial style for many forms of written expression. The distinction, though, is not by any means this clear-cut. It is perfectly possible to write a letter to a family member in a completely colloquial style, and it is equally possible to speak in a literary style, for example in reading a prepared lecture or in giving an unprepared speech on a suitably formal occa-sion. The difference then is not really between spoken and written but between an ordinary, everyday style – itself showing a variety of degrees of casualness – and a formal style which is at a distance from everyone's ordinary way of speaking. This one is used precisely where 'distance' is called for, that is when people interact in a deliberately formalized context in which everything personal is excluded. In other words, we might with some justice say that such situations as these are the true social home of *u* as contrasted with *jij*. These formal situations include newspaper writing, nonfiction and essayistic prose, announcements — even those scrawled in pencil in the door of a dingy shop —, lectures, introductions of speakers and words of thanks and various others. The formal style fulfills an important function in situations in which a person finds it socially desirable to demonstrate written control of the 'proper' forms, but it plays an even more interesting, closely related role in its oral form in certain structured situations. This brings us to one last important rule of the Dutch social game.

Most of us reading this probably feel reasonably accustomed to the type of social situation in which people gather informally for discussion of a certain topic, and get under way by having everyone tell something about himself, after which all proceed, on a first-name basis, to exchange opinions. Such a mode of interaction is foreign to the Dutch, who instead give a great deal of care to formal organization, choosing leaders, purposes and rules for procedure. They operate more comfortably in a network of formalities because they feel that in erecting a certain amount of formal structure they can better ensure the respect of each individual participant's private self. The rules amount to a mutual agreement to touch only the areas understood, so that nobody need feel threatened by overexposure. This type of organization goes by the name *vergadering*, which may be a gathering of two or three people or a large session organized along parliamentary lines. It should come as no surprise to learn that such a formalized situation very readily calls for the formal, 'written' style of speaking, especially in the procedural area itself, the style that signals a comfortable social distance between mutually respectful participants. Nor should it be surprising that *u* is mandatory here, at least in a larger-scale *vergadering*, indeed so much so that in many particularly formal situations the *vergadering* relationship takes precedence over any informal one: a speaker on the rostrum who wants to address an old friend in the·audience is likely to avoid the embarrassment of his customary *jij* and give him a respectful *u*.

In this brief outline we have looked at a few of the more conspicuous dimensions of modern Dutch social life. Different as they may seem at some points, the 'rules' work very well and permit a complex society to progress in a smooth and orderly way without losing control of the many potentially destructive ingredients such as *verzuiling* seems, at first sight, to be. The intense reaction of the society to what was widely interpreted as a violation of a sacred rule, and therefore a threat to its functioning, only serves to underline the deep-seated nature of the rules themselves. The present highly-valued democratic tradition of acceptance is the end result of a long and difficult development, things that took place in the past in what has been called 'an amazing laboratory of social history'.[7] The most logical step at this point is to go back and look for the ways in which the Dutch – or their ancestors – made society work. That they did a great deal more than merely 'make it work' is what makes their past of permanent importance. We will find our first real key to this development toward the end of the Middle Ages.

3 *The emergence of Holland*

There were one or two social circumstances brought up in the previous chapter that reminded us of the rather obvious fact that the Netherlands occupies a very small but densely populated corner of Europe. This very smallness and denseness is interesting in another, more significant way. Anyone who travels around in the present-day Netherlands with anything more than minimum discernment for what he is seeing is sure to be struck by how rapidly he keeps crossing invisible borders into areas where he finds a perceptible difference in outward appearance and, bound up with this, a distinctly different history. If he is able to listen as well, he can hear this same close-knit complex of differences laid down in dialects and regional accents. Even such a small patch of land as the Netherlands must have had numerous separate histories in order to have produced such a patchwork as we can see today. There are constant reminders everywhere of the past grandeur of many of these local histories. To take just one example, The Hague preserves in its official Dutch name *'s-Gravenhage* the memory of Count *(graaf)* William II, who in the middle of the 13th century built, in his relatively insignificant little realm called Holland, a permanent hunting lodge with an enclosure *(haag)* which today is the building in the heart of the city where the national Parliament meets.

It is precisely this colorful and variegated nature of the history of what we now call the Netherlands that makes a study of the past an undertaking of formidable proportions. The further back in time we go, the more history seems to fragment into such a multitude of events all taking place at once that it becomes very difficult to decide which of the many threads to pick up and follow along a ways; it is all but impossible to keep track of everything going on in the area and still retain much sense of historical continuity. In addition to this difficulty we have another serious one: if we find that our search for cultural roots takes us back to the Middle Ages, we find ourselves in a time that may seem more distant than we expected. Life has a different atmosphere, political organizations and the boundaries of states are all different, and causes seem to relate to effects in different ways – it suddenly becomes much more difficult to make sense out of why people did what they did. Since we will need an understanding of what was going on in the Netherlands in this time, we will spend this chapter looking at what actually happened, and then come back in the next chapter to some reflections on why it happened that way.

This leaves us with the problem of which of the many histories we should choose, which of them – if any – represents the most direct line from the generating causes of social organization to the culture we see at work today. If it seems as though the difficulty of sorting out the causes in the distant past are being overemphasized, a comparison of a map of the Netherlands today with one representing the same area in the Middle Ages or in Roman times will demonstrate another awesome fact: even the land itself, its coastline, rivers and lakes become all but unrecognizable. But far from being a troublesome fact, it is just this uniquely intimate relation between a culture and its physical surroundings that makes the cultural history of the Netherlands an unusually challenging one. Romein opens his history *De lage landen bij de zee*[1] with the remark that it is probably true of no other people as it is of the Dutch that the soil it lives on is the foundation of its development and its civilization. From the earliest times the physical makeup of this section of the Northern European coast has presented a challenge to its inhabitants, the response to which is completely interwoven with the evolution of their culture. It is no doubt also symbolic, as Romein also points out, that the very soil of this delta of the Meuse and Rhine rivers is 'borrowed' from somewhere else and transformed here into something different. Armed with a large measure of hindsight derived from our knowledge of history plus the simple fact that the informal name *Holland* in both Dutch and English perpetuates the memory of cultural leadership, we can easily single out the part of this constantly shifting coast that presented the greatest physical challenge and was at the same time in an unusually secure strategic position: the patch of land between, roughly, the outlet of the Zuiderzee in the North to the mouths of the Rhine and the Meuse in the South, the woodlands and shifting marshes behind the row of dunes that gave protection from the sea, the area that in Medieval times turns out to go by the name *Holland.*

It is a fertile but inhospitable country that requires constant vigilance of its inhabitants in order to create at least minimal defenses against the weather, and it is, compared to its neighbors, a culturally backward country that, lacking our hindsight, we would probably hold out little hope for.

When during the course of the eleventh century Holland first enters the stage as an obscure little domain on the fringes of civilization, some of these neighbors (limiting our interest to the lands enclosed within the borders of the present Netherlands and Belgium) have already occupied its center with high cultural achievements. By the year 800 the Carolingian culture to the Southeast has expanded from its heartland between Maastricht, Liège and Aachen to carry its political prestige all the way to Italy and its educational enlightenment to preliterate peoples all over Europe. When this loosely-joined empire fell apart after Charlemagne's death, a three-way split was agreed upon that called for a western realm and an eastern one – the nucleus of the later France and Germany – plus a middle one, that of Lothar, which was called Lotharingen or Lorraine. This middle kingdom did not prove viable, partly because of Lothar's disastrous alliance with the Vikings who for most of a century raided settlements throughout the area. But once in existence, the idea of an indepen-

30

dent middle kingdom forming a counterbalance to the East and the West was one that was destined not to disappear completely.

As life slowly returns to normal after the Viking invasions, in the tenth century we find another cultural renaissance, this time the Romanesque culture that enriches mainly the Meuse Valley to the East. But although this cultural peak too is of great interest for its own sake, both it and the Carolingian renaissance left Holland practically untouched. One reason is the very plain fact, already mentioned, that Holland was not populous enough or advanced enough to carry much weight in these communites of states. The other reason is that Holland still had an only crudely-developed aristocratic class that had little prestige beyond its borders, while both the Carolingian and the Romanesque cultures show all the signs of being the product and expression of a noble elite moving within the tight orbit of a royal or ducal court.

Around 1100 the rulers of this coastal domain – who are not independent but owe feudal allegiance to the distant emperor of Germany – begin calling themselves 'Count of Holland'. The Crusades, in which they participate, have begun stimulating trade all over Europe, and in a rapidly increasing tempo we find enterprising citizens of Holland appearing with their ships in the Mediterranean and in the Orient and serving as merchants to the whole western area. Their enterprise is magnified by the purely geographical circumstance that their homeland lies on the coast, practically forcing them to turn their attention to the sea, and astride the waterways where traffic is increasing almost daily in volume.

Without any doubt, the most important single corollary of this general economic quickening in the 1100's is the rise of cities. In this time, the 'heart' of the Middle Ages, geographical and economic factors combined to produce two separate areas where these remarkable new experiments came into being, Italy in the South and the Lowlands in the North. Trade and industry now called for a more sophisticated

31

type of organization as a response to greater complexity, and the people who answered this challenge found it advantageous to work together in permanent centers where their organizations could be established and defended. A direct and probably inevitable result of this was the fact that new, specifically urban types of social organization came into being. This new class of people was producing unparalleled prosperity and more and more learned to value and exploit the economic power it had in its hand. The commercial leaders everywhere grew into a self-confident class that jealously guarded its rights and its privileged position. As life in the cities came to move at a different tempo from that of the conservative countryside, the cities became increasingly alienated from the country in outlook and in political interest. New and independent systems of government had to be evolved, and new types of laws introduced to regulate unprecedented situations.

Though the economic causes of the development of all these Medieval cities were similar, the Italian cities did not evolve the same political forms as the Northern ones, and in the North we can distinguish several different types of development. If we continue to observe events from our frame of reference in Holland in its early stages of development, looking to the East we see Deventer, Zwolle and Kampen along the IJssel river, cities whose luster goes back to the nobility-focused Romanesque culture and whose present prosperity is based on their membership in the Northern European Hanseatic League. Though at this point they seem rather distant and foreign, being competitors in trade and lying on the other side of the domain belonging to the often antagonistic Archbishop of Utrecht, they make some important cultural contributions we will return to later. Immediately to the South, Gent, Bruges and Ieper (Ypres) in Flanders have already reached a high level of development and therefore of prestige. By the 13th century the economic base of these cities has become so independent of that of the surrounding countryside, controlled by the lower feudal nobility, that a clash of the two divergent interests was inevitable; in addition, another opposition was building up between the rich city aristocracy itself and the class that carried on the trades, organized into guilds. To attempt to trace all the actual expressions of these tensions in historical events would take us too far afield here, but in a word we can say that the new city aristocracy found support from the nominal sovereign, the King of France, while the local nobility tried to maintain what remained of its independence by siding with the guilds. This lengthy struggle culminated in the famous Battle of the Golden Spurs in 1302, the landmark at which for the first time in Europe the new 'middle' class asserted itself and won its independence.

The growing tension between this class and the steadily declining feudal way of life we can see reflected nearly a century earlier in one of the first literary works written in Dutch, the animal epic *Van den vos Reinaerde.*[2] The hero, the fox, continually gets the better of all the other animals, who appear in a typically feudal social organization at the lion's royal court. People are blindly loyal to stupid superiors, the accumulation of 'honor' is carried to the point of absurdity, and the snobbish rabbit even addresses the king in French as a mark of being up with the times. All the bumbling and ineffectual attempts of the animals to subdue the archrogue Reinaert add up to a strong impression that the epic was composed in this 13th-century form for the enjoyment of the newly confident 'middle' class of the Flemish cities.

But the Flemish *Reinaert* epic is considerably more than a simple satire at the expense of one social class. In choosing the form of the epic, with its expertly chosen and paced sequence of 'adventures' that mimic knightly adventures, its stock phrases and characteristically portentious style of introducing persons, objects and events, the unknown author sets up an unfailingly humorous situation. Behind the thin façade of the knightly 'game' they play with such pompous seriousness, the typically animal-like personalities of all the characters constantly assert themselves in a display of absurdity that gives us a clue to what the work is all about. The feudal way of doing things is

33

being viewed as a rigid set of rules, a game that brings out all the vanities and stupidities of which humans are capable, and the fox is not at all a professional rogue but a figure who 'plays the game' to the hilt: he fulfills the expectations of each character in turn and capitalizes in a completely reasonable way on arrogance, stupidity, greed and plain vanity. In spite of his cynical brutality the fox gains and keeps our sympathy, perhaps because he is the only truly free individual, one who plays his role completely and by systematically exploiting all the inherent weaknesses of the game rises above it, only to be forced at the end to take his hard-won independence into disgrace and exile with his family. In a real sense the Flemish *Reinaert* epic is a cultural myth which shows an individual acting in relation to a pervasive game with its established rules. The individual is perhaps the new outlook now beginning to emerge among the prosperous urban merchant classes, and the ultimate message of the story, with all its ambiguities about individual freedom, might well be simply that living in human society means playing a game, ridiculous in many ways but inescapable. This cultural awareness of the tension between play and reality is a trait we will want te keep track of.

The cities of Holland itself developed in much the same way as those of Flanders and the other territories. They evolved the same prosperous and self-confident class and knew the same types of problems. But they significantly underwent their main period of growth just a little later than these neighbors, a circumstance that seems trivial but that has considerable consequences: they emerged into a scene that was another half-century more ready for more progressive developments, such as a more effective coupling of shipping and local industrial development, and that made possible small but pervasive differences in the social climate. The latest developer of them all, in fact, was Amsterdam, which came into prominence in a time that coincided with a new set of political and economic challenges and became the crown over them all.

The emergence of Holland

The same Count William II of Holland who founded The Hague, and who died in battle at the advanced age of 30 trying to subdue his wild northern neighbors, the Frisians, is of more than passing interest to us because he went farther than any other ruler of his time in granting liberties to the rapidly growing cities. These go by the specific name 'privileges', here with quotes to indicate that the meaning is not quite that of our modern English word. 'Privileges' were a specific form of recognition given to a city and its particular laws, and usually took the form of the granting of various kinds of tax exemption and permission to regulate trade, for instance by collecting toll. The granting of 'privileges' was known throughout the Lowlands area, not only in Holland, and the earliest recorded privilege is the customary date of the founding of a city. A document still carefully preserved dates the founding of Amsterdam at 1275, when William's son Count Floris V granted toll privileges to an insignificant village in his dominion. In the 13th century a 'privilege' was thought of as a right to commercial and political gain at the expense of all others, the gathering of as much freedom as possible to take advantage of one's neighbors. 'Privilege' in this sense implied, to a recipient such as an urban unit, independence in the form of strict regulation within but maximum power to impose restrictions on outsiders, and above all exemption from limitations imposed by a central authority. They were thought of as by no means temporary permissions but regarded as permanent, inalienable rights conceded to a city or a state. They were formally drawn up, in this time usually in Latin but increasingly frequently in the vernacular, and provided with the official seal of king, count or duke. Though this somewhat negative concept of 'privilege' may hardly seem to be the base from which the concept of democracy and tolerance is to arise, it is actually a social breakthrough of prime importance. Though the idea itself is originally based on deliberate exclusion of others from a gain, when a whole network of 'privileges' develops the exercisers of all the individual privileges are placed in a type of mutual interaction from which all gain. Besides this, not all privileges imply the disadvantage of someone else, and a concession won by one group is thereafter more easily won by another. In this way people gradually become accustomed to a new style of political life, one in which there develops a complex and closely-organized vying with each other by a number of approximately privileged groups. Though this is still very much a Medieval way or life, its resemblance to certain aspects of modern social life in the Netherlands – *verzuiling* – is obvious and by no means accidental. Documents certifying 'privileges' were scrupulously preserved and appealed to, often centuries later, as the formal claims to political liberty. The increasingly articulate people of the cities, who were the foundation of the prosperity of entire states, demanded and got – though often not without bloodshed – broader and more inclusive 'privileges'. When three centuries later this collection of states found itself absorbed into the Habsburg empire and ruled by its head, the King of Spain, it was this complicated network of highly-prized 'privileges' held as a common heritage that created a chasm between people and monarch whose own people had never heard of 'privileges' and formed the most important single cause of revolt.

All during this 13th century, Holland's increasing prosperity gave it the confidence to expand not only its commercial advantages but its area of physical control. It was a period of turbulent struggles with Friesland to the North and the Bishopric of Utrecht to the East, which resulted in a steady expansion of territory. But the principal rival was Flanders to the South, transformed into an enemy by Holland's dangerously successful commercial expansion. One of the many clashes won Zeeland, a prize contended for by both Holland and Flanders, in 1253, which shared the fortunes of Holland ever after and added the flourishing cities of Middelburg and Zierikzee to Holland's own Leiden, Dordrecht, Haarlem and Gouda. At the very end of the century the crown of Holland and Zeeland was inherited by Henegouwen (Hainaut), a state far to the South, in the present day a province of Belgium, with ways that were so different that the seeds of future tensions were sown.

This same prosperity and confidence enjoyed by the populations of the urban centers created a demand for a literature that would give them pleasure and edification, and that they could understand in their own language. *Van den vos Reinaerde* stands, as we saw, near the beginning of a tradition growing all over Europe, the use of the vernacular for esthetic effect. But the *Reinaert* stands by itself in deliberately satirizing the doings of the feudal nobility. More often what these newly prosperous merchants and administrators demanded was a picture of colorful events tailored to their own needs. In the literature of the 13th and 14th centuries we come across such gems as *Karel ende Elegast,* which transforms history into a pious legend in which Charlemagne follows a puzzling command from God to go out in the middle of the night, and uncovers a plot against him, and *Walewein,* which among other things tells about a knight who goes in quest of a magic chessboard on behalf of King Arthur, and who by exercise of his knightly virtues succeeds in pursuing his goal through a series of bizarre adventures. [3] These and many works like them reflect the tastes of a class of people who loved the grotesque but at the same time wanted a very practical lesson: the good, Christian knight triumphs by scrupulously following the rules set by his religion and his society and is suitably rewarded. This didactic tone sounds throughout the poetic epics and plays written while the knightly ideal was still predominant and providing the primary setting for popular literature. The 33-year reign of Count William III that began in 1304 provided another example of this same 'playful' expression of important realities that will occupy us in the next chapter: it produced, in the midst of a growing social struggle that was to erupt by the middle of the century in years of bitter fighting, a dazzling display of court life which, with its festivals, processions and tourneys, attracted admiring guests from all over Western Europe.

As had been the case in Flanders, this social struggle was the outcome of the increasing distance of interests between the influential merchant patricians of the cities and the nobility that saw its hereditary control being gradually eroded away. The armed conflict that broke out in 1350 was, as practically all Medieval wars, on the surface a disagreement over a succession, but in reality a test of strength of these two antagonistic interest blocs. At this point it might be well to hint at the important difference between a struggle for complete independence from a constituted authority and a struggle for certain concessions that still fully recognized the legitimacy of that authority. The civil war between the *Kabeljauwen* (Cods) and the *Hoeken* (Hooks), the city aristocracy and the nobility, was definitely of the latter sort; even the revolt against Spanish rule two centuries later was not intended, at its outset, to be of the former sort. Both the *Kabeljauwen* and the *Hoeken* supported the claims of the two rival contenders for the succession, and although this question itself was settled soon enough − in favor of the *Kabeljauwen,* which established the power of the merchant aristocrats even more decisively − the succession did nothing to solve the underlying social conflict, and the struggle continued for many years afterward. But this only served to underline with ever more painful clarity who was really on the winning side.

We noted a few pages back that the social history of the cities of Holland was different from that of other cities precisely because these cities developed just a little later, and that this slight delay was of crucial importance. The development of the Italian cities into republics in which the new commercial and political leaders almost immediately assumed all the habits of the old hereditary aristocracy, and the development of the Flemish cities into independent centers run by the guilds, was rapid and tempestuous, and although this development makes exciting reading and produced brilliant cultural expressions, it might be claimed that it was too rapid a buildup to permit permanent assimilation into a viable social structure. Whatever the truth may be, these cities were not able to consolidate their social gains on a permanent basis, and had to watch their experiments in democratic social order wither away again. In the cities of Holland, on the other hand, for all the violence that accompanied social developments, these developments were noticeably more leisurely because the opposing sides did not accumulate enough power soon enough to challenge each other. Since even in the middle of the 14th century these cities were not as economically secure .as the Flemish cities had been a good half-century earlier, they did not provoke a showdown between powerful trade guilds and nobility, but developed a moderately progressive, deliberate business class that slowly expanded its influence on both the political and — perhaps even more significantly — the social level. It can be suggested that this increasing expansion of ways and ideals into further areas of the population was the social consolidation the earlier cities lacked. In any event, the *Kabeljauw* faction seems to have found itself so fully representing the interest of the city populations that it became their effective government, as well as that of the outlying areas that were coming increasingly into the cities' orbits. They evolved into the independent, 'privileged' and often arrogant class of Regents that was later to succeed to complete control.

It now becomes necessary once again to widen our horizon beyond the borders of Holland. Far to the South, in north-central France, an obscure fief of the French crown known as Burgundy was inherited in 1363 by a relative of the king who became the first Duke of Burgundy and who came to be known as Philip the Bold. This distant event becomes of immediate interest to us when we note that by means of a carefully arranged marriage, the customary way of extending one's political claims, Philip acquired Flanders and so gained a foothold in northern lands. This was the first step in a remarkable career of expansion undertaken by Philip and some five generations of successors which transformed Burgundy into a prestigious and powerful state that was able to defy France itself. In 1385 the House of Burgundy acquired control over Hainaut-Holland-Zeeland, a political unit at least in name since 1299, by carefully marrying both his son and his daughter to heirs to these crowns. Since the lands that were thus traded back and forth were thought of in this time as personal possessions of the ruler, the result of such a collection was not a really cohesive empire but a loose confederation in which different peoples, languages and customs continued to go their own way. It was up to the ruler to try to impose as much conformity as he could on his acquired possessions. It happened that the Dukes of Burgundy were keenly interested in consolidating and centralizing their control, something they managed to do with surprising success. It is no accident that the extension of Burgundian control to Holland coincides exactly with the climax of the struggle for power between the *Kabeljauwen* and the *Hoeken:* the fate of the latter, the local nobility feverishly attempting to shore up what remained of its narrow, provincial authority, was sealed when the interests of the Burgundian dukes and the merchant aristocracy turned out to run parallel to each other. Both wanted tranquillity and security throughout a large area in which trade could take place among equally 'privileged' units under a single benevolent authority, and both needed a reduction in the influence of the petty rulers in each area. It was this parallelism that assured the triumph of the regent class and gave them administrative control. But it was also the cooperation of the latter that made Burgundian consolidation possible and so formed a close bond between the cultures of Holland and Burgundy, a fact of great historical importance.

Holland now finds itself incorporated into a new state structure that includes most of what is today the Netherlands and Belgium. However loose-jointed this union may still have been, it is now possible to speak for the first time of 'the Netherlands' rather than of a group of little states in the Lowland region. For all the achievements of the urban merchant aristocracy on the one hand and of Philip the Bold and his son John the Fearless on the other, the real climax of this new cultural fusion is still in the future. By the close of John's reign upon his assassination in 1419, the Burgundians were more and more neglecting their original seat of power in the French city of Dijon in favor of the more illustrious Flemish cities in the northern part of their domains, and when John's son Philip the Good moved his court during his long reign from Dijon to Brussels in the North, the identification of Burgundy with the Netherlands was complete. It should not

40

be surprising that Holland was not the favored place; even by the 15th century it was still a less developed and less glamorous part of the Burgundian realm in spite of the greater coincidence of interest between its political aims and those of the Dukes of Burgundy. And yet it was just this coincidence of interest, the overlapping of some of the most noteworthy achievements of Holland with the main features of Burgundian culture, that was to set the course of future events.

4 The Burgundian ideal

It might not have escaped notice that although the area we know as the Netherlands clearly possessed a very sophisticated form of civilization at least as early as the mid-1200's, the title page talks only of 'six centuries'. The reason is that while it is perfectly true that the states in the Lowlands such as Holland, Flanders, Brabant and Gelderland all participated in the same civilization, on the more specific level of *culture* we might well feel hesitant about using the general term 'Netherlands' quite this early and find ourselves taking refuge in phrases like 'the culture of Holland' as distinguished from 'the culture of Flanders' and so on. It is only in the second half of the 14th century that the cultures of these separate states are overlaid by a cultural stream brought by the new Burgundian sovereigns, to generate something that can rightly be called a culture of the Netherlands. In other words, all that we have considered up to this point is more or less the prelude to the drama that begins at the point where the prospering, urbanized local cultures begin to fuse with a culture originally imported from far to the South. Some of the specific outcomes of this fusion will come to the surface only in later chapters.

In 1419 Philip the Good succeeded his father as Duke of Burgundy, and reigned for almost half a century over the extensive and still expanding Burgundian domains that were at the peak of their cultural achievements. It was under Philip that the name of Burgundy acquired a luster that has never worn off. Philip continued his predecessors' policy of consolidating and centralizing their authority, setting about developing an increasingly complex and efficient central state administration. In 1430 he formalized their growing preference for the North by setting up his official residence in Brussels, where his court attracted not only poets and artists but a great many competent and ambitious administrators. Philip's moves toward a central administrative apparatus for the whole of the Netherlands went a long way toward transforming the task of government from a family-oriented path toward power into a profession, an end in itself. The member states of Philip's realm were each represented before him by a delegation with whom he was obliged to consult on important matters and to whom he had to address his periodic requests for money. It is not hard to guess that it was the urban patricians, the prosperous merchants, who chose these delegates from among their own number; we hear a distinctly 'modern' note, however, in the fact that these delegates did not represent a family or a political faction before the Duke, but rather the abstract idea of their own state including its entire population. Philip found that by joining all these separate provincial delegations together into a single representative body he could save himself the trouble of consulting each one separately, and so the nucleus of a parliament, the later States General, was formed. Still, all was not quite as harmonious and smooth as this may suggest. The Burgundian expansion was not always a matter of judicious dynastic marriages, but authority often had to be imposed by force even in territories that had been gained peacefully, such as the continually rebellious cities of Gent and Bruges. Philip's provinces retained a good share of their accustomed distinctness and their 'privilege'-based independence, and he together with his French-speaking newcomers inevitably came into collision with local jealousies and provincial particularism. The state delegations were exceedingly conscious of their express right to refuse the duke's requests for money, and used this right to exercise control over appointments and public works projects. In spite of this local frustration, Philip was able to assure himself of a constant supply of funds and thus of a permanent state income.

This brief outline of the development of Philip's Burgundy contains the danger to the reader that it makes everything sound much too modern and familiar. It would be a crude anachronism to make it sound as though Philip's state attracted loyalty and enlightened cooperation through devotion to some abstract concept of a national identity. The famous manuscript miniature depicting a scene at the court of Philip might serve to remind us that we are still in the Middle Ages.[1] In a quietly-arranged scene that is so static it seems to have no relation to the focal point of a vigorously growing state, we see Duke Philip in an appropriately ducal pose, dressed in an elaborate hat, fur-lined cloak and pointed shoes and standing under an ornate canopy. Kneeling in front of him on the tiled floor is a figure presenting him with a large book, and the rest of the room is filled with artistically arranged persons whose colorful robes and chains of office show their different functions. Immediately to Philip's left stands his young son Charles, later to become Duke Charles the Bold, and to his right his chancellor. The reminder we need is that the practical business of the state is carried on as something that to contemporaries was only one part of a considerably larger and grander fabric. The miniature gives us a little glimpse at part of an elaborate ritual, the life carried on in what we are tempted to call the 'make-believe' atmosphere of a magnificent court. Philip is not only the formal possessor of his domains; but the essence of them, what makes them all one, somehow resides in his person — how he dresses and acts, how he and his court live, in other words how certain rituals are acted out. It was the outstanding success of the Dukes of Burgundy, but especially of Philip, in combining practical politics with a colorful symbolism that made Burgundian culture into what is probably the clearest expression of the late Middle Ages that can be found. The interesting thing about the tempting term 'make-believe' is that it is so close to the truth, and this leads us back again to the idea that a culture is a type of 'game'.

Our definition of 'culture' in the first chapter was deliberately cast in a somewhat unorthodox way, admittedly in order to provide us with a tool ready for application to present and past stages of Dutch culture alike. We emphasized there that in moving far beyond a rudimentary social response to an environment and creating the explanatory order that is apparently a necessity to human beings, a culture involves its members in a vastly complicated and deadly earnest sort of make-believe. All its manifestations in social arrangement, ritual and artifact are ultimately tied to the fact that its participants say, in effect, 'supposing the system behind appearances to be thus-and-so, our particular ritual reflection of this is right: it shows the working of the system and in fact perpetuates it' – but almost always without knowing that such a hypothesis about the system is only one of many possible. Make-believe is not childish and therefore a stage to be outgrown; it is just that the very thing that distinguishes culture from mere social aggregations is that at one point or another it attempts the formalization of non-rational areas of experience, it marks off the domain of the sacred. It is precisely this underlying arbitrariness of culture, its being in its essence something set aside from ordinary physical reality and yet never turning its gaze away from it, that gives it its striking 'play' aspect. In chapter 2 we began boldly, and very prematurely, to talk about a few of the 'rules' of the cultural game played in the contemporary Netherlands. In actuality, the rules according to which any culture, even a relatively simple one, plays its particular brand of make-believe are exceedingly difficult to isolate and systematize. The difficulty comes in the fact that the rules themselves are abstractions and therefore inaccessible; all we actually have to go by is a mass of more or less accessible outward symbols of these in observable social behavior and material manifestation.

Probably no culture has ever so thoroughly and consistently woven its inner order into its outward manifestation and symbolization as that of the late Middle Ages in Europe. The stylization of all of life into an intricate set of symbolic rules makes almost unavoidable the thought that participants in this culture were engaged in a make-believe on a truly unprecedented scale. This 'game' has been written about many times, but probably most clearly by Huizinga in the two books mentioned in the first chapter, *Waning of the Middle Ages* and *Homo ludens*. It will be well worth our while to pause for a few moments to consider a few of its main characteristics, though from a slightly different point of view than Huizinga.

Medieval culture showed in all its aspects what strikes us today as a curiously static quality. The world was made up of a stupendous array of things, relations and events, all of them distinct from each other and each possessed of its own unique individuality. Scholastic thought, for instance, was thoroughly permeated with the idea that the most complicated and subtle problems could be dealt with by arranging everything into the appropriate sealed compartments, and by discovering the general principles according to which these separate entities interacted with each other. Each thing, event, or person was 'what it was', and the way the culture set about presenting the world to its participants was to prompt them to ask what the purpose was behind appearances, in other words WHY things are rather than the modern HOW things are. The question could be asked in this way, and only in this way, because of one very important aspect to this collection of independent things: man knew them in part, in time, whereas God knew them in eternity, which is another way of saying that each and every thing and event had its own divine aspect, it symbolized something eternal beyond itself and ultimately mysterious to man. No matter how trivial a thing or an event may have been, it had its own sacred quality, it meant something, and had to be treated in accordance with this individual eternal meaning. The logical obverse of this coin is that everything can be expressed by the choice of the proper symbol — in fact, it could not be expressed in any other way in order to be graspable to the mind. The working out of the exquisitely complicated system of relations between the world of appearances and the meanings of these was one of the dominant institutions of Medieval culture, one that came to full ripeness in the 15th century but whose rigidity ultimately spelled the end of the culture's vitality. Even in this 15th century, as Huizinga points out on many occasions, the game of symbols becomes so pervasive that the healthy distance between seriousness and play is threatened: too great a readiness to believe in the awesome importance of even the most trivial erodes a common-sense feeling for the legitimate limits of make-believe.

The most absorbing facet of Medieval culture is the way it chose to symbolize itself. The means for giving expression to this culture were in the hands of an adequately leisured class that had its home in the numerous courts, large and small, and that was highly homogeneous throughout Europe. The symbolism through which this courtly class saw itself was focused on what has come to be known as the knightly ideal — an image that modern times have so romanticized that it is almost impossible to recover its meaning to Medieval culture. In rough and unsettled times the knights had a very real social function in keeping roads and bridges open and relatively safe and in protecting the innocent from intolerable injustice. In a more stable society and a more complicated economy they found themselves increasingly super-fluous, but because each thing was 'what it was' and not something else, their culture left them no flexibility, and probably a much greater percentage of them would have turned into outlaws except for the happy circumstance that the culture turned them into symbols that were vital to its functioning. They became indispensable once again because in their normal activity and in their increasingly elite role at the courts they had evolved some important rules for behavior toward others, strictly circumscribed and stylized forms of what we still call 'courtesy', a word that still has 'court' embedded in it. These rules included, and in fact were grouped around, a new attitude toward women which removed them from the category of possessions and turned them into an important focus for mannerly behavior. With the perspective of centuries we now think we can see that the knight in riding out in search of adventure was really looking for the dimensions of his own self and symbolically slaying the age-old dragons of fear and the unknown; all that we need to see at the moment is that the Medieval tales about knights say over and over, in an ingenious variety of ways, that whoever — in the person of the 'knight' — follows scrupulously the moral forms his culture lays down its interpretation of his religious call will unavoidably succeed completely. The courtly culture which thus walled itself off in a glass cage and evolved a cultural expression for all participants to follow succeeded in holding at bay all harsh reality and unaccountable failure. A classic example of what we mean by cultural 'make-believe'. The rules developed by this culture gave a central place to the approval of society, the accumulation of 'honor' satirized in the *Reinaert.* The numerous epic poems it produced, many of them originally written in France and then translated and expanded all over Europe, show the great importance attached to the observance of proper form, not only in manners but in the colorful forms of conspicuous consumption such as festivals, costumes, and tourneys of precisely the sort that made the court of Count William III of Holland so famous. Though William's court life may have seemed to us before to be ignoring urgent reality in favor of a game, we can now see somewhat more clearly that this display had its indispensible symbolic value to everyone, including the majority of the society that did not directly participate. It was just this symbolic function that was filled for one final time by the Dukes of Burgundy.

In personal wealth, the Dukes of Burgundy were second only to the Italians. Their extensive dominions were, as we noted, their personal possessions from which they could draw profit as they saw fit. Philip did not invent any courtly display but simply inherited it and continued 'playing the game'. Though he demanded efficient organization and tolerated no nonsense, he loved luxury and maintained a court life that in some aspects looks like an anticipation of that of Louis XIV two centuries later. There were ceremonies and processions, people dressed, in keeping with the universal custom of the time, in distinctive ways that showed their function — 'what they were' — and the forms of courtly behavior had to be followed by anyone who expected to rise higher. In this way a system of rules supported by the culture — including the patricians who, as we saw, demanded knightly tales with a moral — tended to mold members of the culture in its own form and so perpetuate itself. In 1430, the year of his move to

Brussels, Philip founded the Order of the Golden Fleece. This act was typically Medieval in that it was exclusively symbolic, the order serving no specific function whatever other than providing a visible index to the key participants in Philip's courtly society and of course strengthening their personal loyalty to him. The members wore scarlet robes trimmed with sable and the golden chain that can be seen on the shoulders of Philip's son Charles in the portrait by Rogier van der Weyden. [2] The procession in Bruges that marked the inauguration of the Order is said to have lasted two hours and to have included nobles from various lands, many courtiers including the painter Jan van Eyck, dignitaries from the German Hanseatic League and merchants from Italy. Visible manifestations like these were tangible evidence to the viewers that the key symbol of all the complicated symbolism of life was indeed functioning in the proper fashion: the robes represented the persons in their roles as places in an immutable hierarchy. By thus presenting society with the cultural image it expected, the Dukes of Burgundy welded together their realm in a way that was a harmonious complement to conquest and political manipulation. In a very real way everyone did in fact participate in Philip's courtly display, because everyone was trained by his culture how to interpret its symbolic meaning.

Surely nothing could be more natural than to see Van Eyck, the master of brilliant color whose eye missed nothing, taking part in the life of a culture that loved colorful display and that would certainly have valued his ability to capture its wealth of symbolic detail. While this is in fact true, it was due to his unique genius, and we still ought to be a little surprised to find him being given a status equal to these dignitaries. The contemporaries of Van Eyck did not quite agree with our modern view that the quintessence of late Medieval culture is nowhere better captured than in painting; they regarded painters as little better than decorators and instead felt that their poets, whose works are known today only to a few specialists, were the real artists who therefore deserved an honored place at court. Painters had been quietly working for centuries at their modest task of decorating manuscripts with miniature paintings, and it was precisely in the Netherlands that these decorators developed their technique of compressing a wide range of color and a seemingly endless amount of detail into a very small space, turning a trade into a high art. Gradually they came to be called on to do larger-scale works; an example that immediately comes to mind is the famous Book of Hours of the Duc de Berry with its paintings taking up most of a page. When the characteristic Medieval love of bright color and display was coupled with Burgundian wealth and ostentation, painting came into its own as a natural means of expression and the decorators were given increasingly more challenging tasks to fulfill, culminating in the one that for sheer control of color and breadth of horizon was never to be surpassed: Van Eyck's Adoration of the Lamb, done in 1431 for the altar of the St. Bavo in Gent and today still to be seen there.

These painters are usually called the Flemish Primitives, and in fact the names we are most likely to find in art histories – Rogier van der Weyden, Hugo van der Goes, Hans Memlinc or Quinten Massijs – are all those of southern painters. But even though they, like the contemporary political elite, represent what we think of as Belgium rather than the Netherlands, there is not yet any cultural distinction between North and South, and these painters are every bit as much the ancestors of the later culture of the Netherlands as northern painters such as Geertgen tot Sint Jans, Lucas van Leiden and Jan van Scorel. The genius of all these painters was the same. Their centuries-old craft of illumination has prepared them to see keenly and accurately and miss not a single detail, while their Medieval culture has taught them the equal symbolic importance of even the most trivial thing. Many of them traveled to Italy and were admired there for their breathtaking ability to put down bright color and represent every hair and thread; in Italy the bold new techniques of the Renaissance were being taught, and although the Flemish did not step into the new era with its intense individuality and its sweeping arrangement, they at least faced in its direction when they opened up the Medieval flat surfaces and created perpective and space. The spectacular success of the

Flemish Primitives in learning how to give visual representation to even the most trivial thing in such a way as to suggest its eternal, sacred quality is plainly evident in almost any of the works produced in the Lowlands in the 14th and 15th centuries. But in a peculiar way their paintings usually have a way of failing to cohere in a single impression but seem to fall apart into a collection of many individual close observations. Thus the genius of the Lowland painters in treating each idea independently and with scrupulous faithfulness seems to have denied them a sure grip on the elusive quality of visual unity. We must find this unity not so much in the Renaissance's single visual impression as in a collective symbolic impression that we get – as did the contemporary viewer – through knowledge of a whole system of symbols.

It has become customary to claim for Van Eyck, perhaps more than for any of his contemporaries, the distinction of having been able to achieve both a symbolic and a visual unity at the same time. Rather than considering one of his more restrained paintings such as the highly symbolic portrait of Jan Arnolfini and his bride, let us deliberately select a painting in which the wealth of detail threatens to crowd out the symbolic unity of the whole. Such a painting is the one called the Madonna of Canon Van der Paele, painted as part of an altarpiece for the Church of St. Donatian in Bruges. The Madonna and child are seen in the center of the painting, seated serenely in a stylized pose on a throne in a church. Both figures are turned slightly toward a kneeling figure on the right side of the painting whose white robe stands out vividly against the rather subdued colors of the whole. This is Canon Van der Paele, an ecclesiastical official of considerable importance in the Burgundian administrative hierarchy and the commissioner of the painting. He holds in his hands several small articles that symbolize his office, in addition to a pair of spectacles that indicates realistically one of his minor infirmities. So unsparingly has the artist rendered the hard, unforgiving lines of his fleshy face in the bright light that he steals a considerable amount of our attention away from the Madonna. He is being presented to her by St. George, his patron saint, who appears in armor at the right side of the painting; he is holding a banner, the staff of which makes a diagonal line accentuating several elements of the composition such as the plane of the Madonna's head and right arm holding the infant. At the left stands St. Donatian himself, holding the wheel with candles that signals his claim to sainthood: as a child he had fallen into the water, and a wheel with candles floated to where he was to be found, enabling him to be rescued. St. Donatian is a bishop, and the brilliant blue velvet of his robe trailing on the floor forms a delicately-poised balance to the red of the Madonna's robe. Except for the fact that Van der Paele tends to attract the eye to himself, all the figures are arranged in such a way that they form a harmonious and logical group. The light coming in from an invisible source at the left bathes the whole scene in a perfectly clear but mellow illumination making the figures stand out and other details recede somewhat into the background. Nevertheless, the eye finds it rather difficult to stop at this point, and continues wandering over the painting noticing increasingly more significant detail. There is an intricate design in the rug leading up to the throne and covering almost equally intricately-ornamented floor tiles; the little sculptures on the armrests of the throne are clearly discernable, as are the carvings on the capitals of the columns forming an arcade behind the figures. This search for detail reaches almost bizarre proportions: the artist has faithfully rendered the slightly worn effect of the rug as it passes over the edges of the steps, and the saints woven into the glittering gold brocade of St. Donatian's robe, though tiny, are so distinct that we can see the realistic folds of *their* robes and find ourselves peering closer to see whether perhaps they, in turn, might have little saints woven ino the ornamentation of their robes! Though the figures, the colors, the many articles and even the Romanesque rather than Gothic architecture of the church all have their assigned symbolic function, and though in this context no detail is too insignificant for the painter's eye, it is all held together, albeit perhaps precariously, by the almost living quality of the light that unites all the elements into a single impression. For our modern feeling there is a tension between abstract symbolism and concrete

52

realism, the latter constantly endangering the cohesion of the former, but for the contemporary who by viewing the painting participated in it, Van Eyck's technical feat so well represented the sense of his world full of unquestioningly accepted and revered ordinary things that it is with perfect justice that this artist is often singled out as the foremost communicator of late Medieval culture. A practically-oriented visual acuteness was to be a characteristic of the culture of the Netherlands for a long time to come.

Hieronymus Bosch was born after Van Eyck was already dead, and when we recall his scenes of horror and nightmare that seem to be attempting to pull back the veil of the familiar we might think of him as belonging to a different era or culture. But Bosch too is not only Medieval in his love of the grotesque as symbolic of the evil lurking throughout the world, but a Netherlander in his minute attention to the importance of each detail. Nothing is too small for his eye, though this eye sees far different significance in things than did those like Van Eyck who captured a cool serenity that belied the chaotic quality of much of Medieval life. It is not the specific interpretation at all but the ability to place an array of persons and things in a setting in which everything has its meaningful and proper place, the feeling for all the trivial parts of a whole, that makes for what we can more and more distinguish as a uniquely Netherlands way of viewing the world. This quality is apparent for all to see in the work of Pieter Brueghel, who in turn was born after the death of Bosch and did his work a full century after Van Eyck. Everyone is familiar with his paintings, so full of movement that the figures often look like insects rather than people. It would be wrong to stop with the idea that he gave vivid expression to peasant life in the 16th century, however successfully he did this; he showed men doing various things, often trivial and everyday things, fully immersed in their natural settings. Even if we have to consider him still Medieval because of the stubbornly static quality of most of his paintings viewed as wholes, he certainly stands at the threshold of the Renaissance in presenting people as real, flesh-and-blood actors in the scenes and not mere symbolic figures. He is a Netherlander too: in his grandly-conceived spaces everything and everyone has a function and a place, and nothing happens divorced from its rightful setting. Everything within this setting is observed and recorded with devoted attention — it has a sacredness precisely by virtue of its being the context in which life is carried on.

It may seem as though we have spent an undue amount of time considering Medieval culture in the Netherlands, a period that in a sense is only a preparation for the real flowering of culture that comes in the early 17th century. The reason why we have lavished so much of our attention on a distant period which admittedly is relatively similar all over Western Europe is that in an important sense Netherlands culture acquires a feature here that it never really abandons again. This is precisely the devotion to the everyday and the raising of its details to a high level of significance that we have found to be so characteristic of Medieval culture. The culture of the Netherlands learns to observe carefully the parts of the whole, and when it leaves the Middle Ages it transforms this habit and gives it new meaning. When in the middle of the 19th century we watch the writer Nicolaas Beets describing Dutch family life in loving detail, it is almost as if we were watching a latter-day Van Eyck painting with words instead of pigments.

The translation of the word *herfsttij* in Huizinga's title as 'waning' must have caused someone a certain amount of hesitation. Huizinga's own suggestive image would have been more accurately rendered by the clumsier 'autumn season' or the like, something that would communicate the image of a late blaze of brilliant color that by its very mellowness and sadness signals an approaching end. The colorful Burgundian era gave expression to the Medieval symbolic world one final time, and used the knightly ideal as its central theme just before it lost completely its own symbolic appeal in the late 15th-century world that refused to fit its pattern. This was one part of what we might call the Burgundian ideal, but it had another important ingredient that was equally significant in setting the course toward political unity and that now found itself swallowed up in the changing political tides of the end of the 15th century. This was the ideal of Burgundy itself, the successor to the ancient Lorraine and the powerful, independent middle kingdom that had as its main reason for being the creation of a political rival to the French crown. This was the ideal that guided Philip in his career of expansion, and it was continued to an almost fanatical degree by his successor, Charles the Bold. The portrait that serves as Huizinga's frontispiece shows no longer a Medieval knight but a Renaissance prince, proud, severe, brooding and ruthlessly ambitious. In his ten-year reign, Charles pursued a reckless policy of continued expansion and centralization that increased the financial burdens on the people who had to support him with money, and greatly widened the already increasing gulf between him and the local government officials. By the time he died he left behind a state that was in disarray and showing more and more signs of discontent. The rest of the story up to where we will again take up the historical thread in Chapter 6 can be told briefly: when Charles was killed Burgundy was immersed in a war with France; in desperation his daughter Mary had to call on the States General, which supported her only after she had agreed to a number of concessions limiting her power. Soon after this, she was married to Maximilian of Austria, the son of the emperor of Germany. When Maximilian later became emperor, Burgundy became another state in the vast Habsburg empire and accordingly permanently separated from France. In the hard realities of political turmoil, the struggle between the increasingly powerful monarchy on the one hand and the increasingly independent, 'privileged' Netherlands provinces on the other, the last of the make-believe of the old Burgundian game evaporated. The son of Mary was another Philip, called Philip the Fair, who married a Spanish princess and produced a son Charles, born in Gent in 1500; Charles became King of Spain as Charles V and in 1519 was elected emperor of Germany, which made him head of the Habsburg empire at its peak. Though the Habsburgs developed the habit of leaving the Netherlands to be governed by a regent, usually a close relative, Charles helped to close the administrative gap between the regent and the local government by the creation of a Council of State which gave

Netherlanders a certain voice in the decision-making process. In 1555 Charles was physically worn out and he abdicated, turning over the throne to his son, yet another Philip, who was born in Spain and who now became King Philip II. By Charles' side as he pronounced his abdication in Brussels was a young court favorite of his, a German prince named William of Orange.

While we have come to the end of an era with the Netherlands submerged in the Habsburg empire, life in the cities of the North has been growing and evolving new forms that are to provide the vital response to the social challenges to come. We can understand these best by pausing here to consider an area we have neglected, that of religion and general outlook on life — *levensbeschouwing.*

5 *The birth*
of a new symbolism

Medieval culture at its height around 1200 was, for its participants, a harmonious and well-integrated interpretation of the world: all of life is strictly divisible into the sacred and the profane, into eternal and temporal, but these two opposites are intimately interwoven with each other in that everything profane has a mysterious sacred aspect while sacred things have profane things to stand for them as symbols. A powerful central church at the peak of its influence and prestige was the final arbiter in all that concerned the sacred realm and thus entered thoroughly into all aspects of ordinary life. This was all the more true because this cultural manipulation of symbols carried with it a rigid belief in established authority, the Bible coupled with Aristotle, which perpetuated itself in the schools run by the church.

But even in the course of the 1200's the outstanding success of this cultural response was showing signs of crumbling. The church organization itself became too rigid to respond to new challenges from the nobility and, later, from the emerging 'third estate'; the humiliating 'Babylonian Captivity' of the pope in Avignon coincided with the clash between nobility and third estate at Courtrai (the 'Golden Spurs') and went on until the last quarter of the 14th century, leaving a weakened and demoralized central authority. Inseparable from this – whether as cause or as effect is impossible to say – is the perhaps more ominous fact that the symbolic interpretation of the world is itself steadily losing its force. Life becomes so filled with religion, everything becomes so top-heavy with sacred import, and religious traditions multiply to such an extent, that a once meaningful cultural expression of an underlying world view becomes meaningless and turns into an undiscriminating, rote observation of the surface forms. This points to a cultural breakdown, which we find evidence of in a marked increase in disrespect for ecclesiastical authority and for the cultural institution it represents, a great increase in attraction to the fantastic and grotesque, and a huge increase in the departure from established norm that the church labeled heresy. If we could explain just how this cultural crisis came about, where the new challenges to authority came from, we would go a long ways toward accounting for the Renaissance itself. But an appropriate modesty of objective that keeps our horizon restricted to the way the cultural game is played in the Netherlands will at least give us a fair chance of tracing down some of the ways it happened there.

It seems certain that the key to the rejection of tradition and the questioning of its authority is to be found, in the Netherlands just as in Italy, in the evolution of a self-confident urban culture that developed its own distinct patterns of life and therefore new types of cultural response to its unique challenges. Though heresy cropped up all over Europe in the Middle Ages, it was always a particularly stubborn problem in the Lowlands where many aspects of the pre-Christian religions had been submerged but never completely obliterated; some types of 'uncivilized' religious ritual began reasserting themselves in the thirteenth, fourteenth and fifteenth centuries, and called into being the Inquisition. A more significant phenomenon, a general manifestation of Western European culture that took especially strong root in the Lowlands, was the emergence of Mysticism. The mystics responded to the increasing emptiness and rigidity of the traditional system of symbols not by transforming them into new and unaccustomed forms but by allowing all of them to recede and fade away in a direct, symbolless relation between the individual and a central religious truth. This emphasis on inwardness and the ultimate significance of the response of the individual constantly brought them up to the border or heresy and often across it, but gradually they became the voice of religious renewal, having found a fresh way of moving within the old symbolic pattern. The uninterrupted line of these independent interpreters of religious experience from Hadewijch down to Ruysbroeck and Thomas a Kempis would seem to indicate that they found a fertile ground in the urbanized culture of the Netherlands.

The Burgundian Netherlands contained an area that in the 13th and 14th centuries was second only to Flanders in prosperity and independence: the flourishing Hanseatic trade centers Deventer, Zwolle and Kampen strung out along the IJssel River which leaves the Rhine valley and flows northward, at that time giving immediate access to the North Sea. Here, almost on the edge of the Burgundian horizon, the flourishing of commerce that was founded on hard-won privileges once again stimulated the growth of a polite, practical and self-assured city culture that valued order, propriety, regularity and a reasonable social acceptance of those with whom one might disagree — all the virtues that are essential to a sophisticated business community with international connections.

The first strong voice of this urban culture in answer to a crumbling and confused feudal society and to a church trapped in a suffocating feudal organization was that of Geert Grote, born in Deventer in 1340. [1] He came to be so disturbed by the increasing meaninglessness of religious symbols that were merely imposed from above that he abandoned his successful career as a scholar and began preaching. His command of the spoken word had an impact on a scale it is difficult to imagine in an age thoroughly oriented to the more detached written word, and he attracted such a large following that eventually the ecclesiastical authorities saw fit to forbid him to preach. His considerable stature as a cultural innovator lies, however, not in this talent but in the uncommon penetration of his insight that the religious symbolism he witnessed could only produce fear and anxiety in a culture that had lost sight of its original, more profound significance. Like all religious reformers everywhere, he reasoned that unless religious observance was an expression of an inner understanding of what the culture was trying to say to its members about their ultimate place in the order of things, it was without any value whatever. He looked around him and found this to be true of the whole system of consecration of priests, vows and monastery life, and so with scrupulous consistency he bypassed it all and founded a house in Deventer where religious seekers could escape from the vanity of everyday life to search, in an atmosphere without formal rules and outward restrictions, for quiet and meaning. In his preaching and in the advice he gave to the large numbers of people who during the course of years came into contact with him, Geert Grote constantly focused on a single theme: the only true test of whether you are following the right course is to search your own experience and see whether the central religious principles are really alive there. Although he rejected the entire tradition of Scholasticism with its endless hair-splitting about mere words and both preached and wrote against meaningless church rules, he was not a revolutionary but, for all his independence, remained a faithful, heresy-conscious servant of the church. The *Broederschap des gemenen levens,* the 'Brotherhood of the Common Life' that was his personal creation, was an unquestionably Medieval organization that drew on the same inspiration as the Mystics, but its real difference is that it was an unambiguous expression of the urban culture of Deventer. Its outlook on the religious life was reasonable, matter of fact, practical, even businesslike, putting into practice Geert Grote's belief that a sane, rational interpretation of inner experience was the best guide to religious truth. This rationalism has practically no similarity to that of the 18th century that sought to replace religion, but instead assumes the role of respiritualizing a system whose essential rightness is never questioned. Thus Geert Grote was the spokesman of the citizenry of the Northern cities, who were disturbed by the ease with which monastic vows could be forgotten in the midst of the temptation they offered and who needed a cultural symbolism that better reflected their own confident new style of life.

Geert Grote, the 'last Medieval man' as Romein calls him, hastened the breakdown of the Medieval game by turning its array of symbols into a demand for inner understanding that threatened to break through the boundaries of the old symbolic system. When he was forbidden to preach, he turned his energy to the defense of his order, which was being vigorously attacked, but also to its spiritual encouragement, which took the form of personal advising and translation of religious works into the vernacular – one of which most likely served as the forerunner of the well-known *Imitation of Christ,* usually ascribed to his follower Thomas a Kempis. After his death at the age of 44 his new-style religious order spread until there were communities throughout the Netherlands perpetuating a new urban answer to the problem of giving meaning to cultural symbols.

The step from the last Medieval man to the first modern one is an unexpectedly short one. It was probably in 1469 that the same Burgundian Netherlands – though now increasingly urbanized – saw the birth, in Rotterdam, of Desiderius Erasmus, who began by studying for the priesthood and was educated by . . . the Brothers of the Common Life. [2] Erasmus absorbed from them a sense for order and reason and came to be filled with Geert Grote's own vision of a new, inner response to the cultural crisis he witnessed. But Erasmus had a different personality, and he was born into a world that in a century had changed in significant ways. Erasmus had a shy, hesitant personality that abhorred all aggressiveness, and a fastidiousness and love of order that marked him as a perfect example of a product of urban culture. His lifelong search for reason and refinement was certainly an urge that had its origin in his upbringing, and his illegitimate birth may have some connection to a certain defensiveness that always sought out the middle ground and was never quite satisfied. It was probably this same urge for refinement that led him to the camp of those who spurned the vernacular and took refuge in the expressive potentialities of Latin, his medium of written communication throughout his life. But although Humanism, which began in an impulse in the prosperous Italian cities to recover the glory of their past, was superficially a movement that did indeed have as its main goal the development of Latin eloquence, to Erasmus it meant far more than this. Where Italian Humanism was largely a philological matter, for Erasmus it was an ethical one that brought scholarship into its service.

One feature all the Humanists had in common was an intense antagonism to Medieval Scholasticism, which they regarded as a thoroughly artificial system of preconceived symbols imposed on what should be a free human spirit. In its place they proposed to let this spirit emerge by recapturing the harmony and elegance of Classical civilization and expressing its creativity in linguistic eloquence, which meant in Latin – a fateful step, taken at the very moment the vernaculars were coming into their own, which sent the Humanists up an unfortunate blind alley. For the Northern Humanists, the importation of this ideal coincided with a profound dissatisfaction with the state of religious belief, and Humanism came to be identified with religious reform. Although Erasmus wrote a large number of popular works dealing with the development of eloquence in Latin, showing how many ways there really were of expressing one's thoughts, his real mission all through his life was pursuing the ideal that he found in Antiquity as well as in the scriptures: residing in all men there is a kernel of wisdom and reason that is the ultimate gauge of rightness and that is not capturable by any one set of rules, although it was given fullest development in Antiquity and in Christianity. His program of education accordingly involved a concentration on humane, ethical behavior, showing people how this inner dimension of the personality might be developed into a true religious guide. It is this bold step casting aside the old symbolic system entirely that makes Erasmus modern; though he is usually accused of being timid where his contemporary Luther was courageous, the judgement of history may be turning in his favor: it was Luther who was conservative in emphasizing grace at the expense of free will and in defending the 'real' church, and Erasmus who struck out boldly in throwing away all outer authority and presuming to depend solely on each man's individual free will.

Erasmus, who wanted more than anything else to reconcile all religious conflicts by showing the spaciousness of the common ground of meaningful belief, lived in a time .that was not quite ready for this, and he was attacked by both Catholics and Protestants, the first for his radicalness and the second for his conservatism. The Erasmian age did arrive, but by then it was only his influence that was still alive.

The fact that Erasmus was an internationally known figure, that he spent most of his adult life outside the Netherlands and that he wrote exclusively in Latin always masks the important fact that he remained in heart and soul a Netherlander, or more specifically a Hollander. In the value he places on order, honesty, reasonableness and polite behavior toward one's fellow men we can easily see the virtues valued by a businesslike city population, and his insistence in many works on the practical worth of the behavior he urges is the voice of one who has been taught the importance of practical utility. The Burgundian Netherlands had a widely diffused cultural ideal of moderation and enlightened, polite behavior which was fast becoming the distinguishing characteristic of the new 'middle' class; Erasmus' opposition to Luther's Reformation bears distinct marks of a bourgeois reaction to the crude behavior of an unmannerly peasant. 'Home' to Erasmus was the province of Holland, which contained both Rotterdam and the monastery of Steyn near Gouda, from which all his life he was technically on temporary leave. The blend of urbane sophistication, common-sense practicality and didacticism that Erasmus made his own is nowhere more clearly apparent than in the *Praise of Folly,* by far the most popular and at the same time the most Dutch of all his works.

In the *Praise of Folly* we are guests at a banquet or drinking party of the sort familiar in Antiquity, and find ourselves participating in the conviviality by listening to a good-humored oration made by the goddess Folly herself. She opens the oration with the claim that she is the deity who recreates both gods and men, that indeed she is the most universal of all the gods. It is easy to picture Erasmus' enjoyment as he now gives Folly free rein for some sophisticated fun at the expense of the Ancients, but fortunately understanding of these barbs is not essential for appreciation of the work. Everywhere in life, she says, real enjoyment comes only through having recourse to Folly. Of course children are foolish, as are adults in producing them in the first place — here even the gods themselves throw aside their dignity — and if everyone could learn to renounce pompous wisdom and cling to Folly, they could enjoy perpetual youth. Then they could enjoy the gross, simple things of life, a skill managed best of all by her friends . . . the Hollanders! It is foolishness of this sort that blinds people to the faults of those they love and so glues society together. Not only unreasoned love of others is good, she continues, but vain self-love as well — the foolish love of glory that keeps the arts flourishing. Let us not only admit that we play-act all the time, but in fact embrace this as something sublime and vital to the functioning of life. If someone should come up on the stage and strip the costume off a player, proudly showing him 'as he really is', would he not deserve to be driven off the stage with stones? Here we have what seems to be Erasmus' point: all of life is a kind of counterfeit, a comedy, a game without which there is no real living. There is nothing more foolish (note that our orator is an accomplished rhetorician and has now slyly used the word in an opposite sense) than the wisdom that sets up its own fancied truths in disregard of the common sense truth gotten from life itself. Would its idea of the perfect man, she asks, be able to live? No; someone who could not have common feelings because he could not make mistakes would be like a stone statue and nobody could stand to have him around. Having convinced us that folly is wisdom, Folly has now begun showing us that wisdom is folly, but she has switched the sense of the words so subtly that we are hardly aware of where the change took place. She now parades a variety of kinds of learning before her audience, only to tear down both secular and sacred with her merciless humor as foolish. All, not excepting the Pope himself, miss the true spirit of Christian life to the extent that they insist on taking the scriptures with sober and heavy seriousness: its essence is its being a new brand of foolishness, and its example is Christ himself who took on the nature of a fool. This alliance with folly is its life and happiness – its shows people how to live. By this time the listeners may be forgiven for wondering whether Folly, who has been telling us not to take ourselves too seriously, isn't taking her own message a little too seriously. No, she suddenly says, as if anticipating this thought, this whole oration has been spoken by a mere foolish woman, and she now remembers nothing of what she has said. Furthermore, she hates people who insist on remembering what was said over the cup. So go forth, she says, and live foolishly.

The *Praise of Folly* should be of considerably more than passing interest to us in our quest for cultural themes. Here we have, at the very beginning of the modern era, a member of the culture of the Netherlands announcing to the world that the essence of a sane life in society is to be found in foolish playing, in a priceless sort of 'make-believe'. In other words we are not immersed in a labyrinth of symbols which we manipulate in predetermined ways as slaves, but rather we stand off detached from the profoundest things and try on various costumes to see which image our eternally changing spirit likes best. It is only in this 'foolishness', this freedom from the suffocating rigidity of the Medieval interpretation of everything, that the divine creativity of the human spirit can be given room. There is no one single, unalterable truth to be handed down, and fanatics of every stripe are to be abhorred. The truth comes from what settles out of this constant game played by society that allows individuals to find it by living with each other on the practical level. Erasmus was probably the first one in modern times to perceive the vital importance, in a healthy adjustment to life, of the ability to see that things could be different, the realization of the underlying absurdity of all our make-believe that today we call a sense of humor. What makes the *Praise of Folly* a great work of art is the graceful way in which Erasmus weaves the message of his work into its style: in speaking through Folly he is playing a whimsical game that leaves us perpetually wondering where the serious point really is, whether we should take Folly seriously or, if not, whether we are then to believe the opposite of all she says, and

65

whether we are to take seriously or as foolishness Erasmus' high-handed pulling out of the rug at the very end. However this may be, a number of aspects of the culture developing in Holland have combined to leave us with an image of a great game of give-and-take within which one finds his true self.

Erasmus' sharp consciousness of the play element in human life and his conspicuous ability to evoke persons and scenes vividly in words — especially evident in his second best known work, the *Colloquies* — may have influenced many who put these same interests into practice in the vernacular, or they may have provided ideas for him, but most likely Erasmus' career and the cultural creativity of the contemporary *Rederijkers* were both parallel developments with much in common. These 'Chambers of Rhetoric' emerged on the scene in the 15th century as part of the Medieval guild structure and evolved during the course of the 16th century into important formers and transmitters of literary and artistic culture with a stamp that is peculiar to the Netherlands. This is as much as to say that they were significant 'mythmakers' for their culture.

The *Rederijkers* were characterized throughout their history by typical Medieval play elements — the name itself is a pun originating with the Latin *rhetorica* — such as elaborate ceremony, costumes, processions and, above all, rules. Their purpose was primarily the creation and performance of verses and plays, an occupation which as time went on led them into the area of cultivation of the mother tongue. In the process of creating lyrics and developing stagecraft and visual effects for their dramas, they found themselves pursuing a more varied and expressive form of the vernacular on the more theoretical level. For them *rhetoric,* one member of the Medieval Trivium which also included grammar and dialectic, was the chief of all the branches of human knowledge, the one in which man's true, individual nature was most genuinely expressed and the one that most the most valuable to society: it is in our purposeful and effective using of our language that we find ourselves, and when this using is formalized and stylized according to definite rules, we play a game that has analogies to society itself. The purest form of such a linguistic undertaking is, not surprisingly, the play.

The most famous of all the plays that owe their existence to the *Rederijkers* is *Mariken van Nieumeghen*,[3] the oldest surviving version of which dates from around 1500. Mariken is an orphan who lives with her uncle, a priest. She is sent to the city to go shopping, after which she visits her aunt, who however treats her insultingly and abusively. In her despairing mood she is befriended by Moenen, who in reality is the Devil himself. He persuades her to join him in a life of adventure, and changes her name to Emmeken, a diminutive form of the letter M. In Antwerp, a big city full of glamorous temptations, they create all sorts of mischief. After some six years of this life Emmeken feels uneasy and urges Moenen to take her back to Nijmegen - where, unknown to her, her uncle has been praying daily for her all this time. On their return they notice that a play is being produced on a street corner. It turns out to be about the fall and redemption of man, and while watching it Mariken is seized with remorse and insists that the Devil release her. He responds by throwing her from a great height down onto the street, but she survives and is recognized by her uncle, who was watching the same play. He disposes of Moenen by reading off the appropriate incantation, and takes Mariken off to help her gain absolution. This is finally granted by the Pope himself, who imposes penance on her in the form of heavy iron rings to be worn on her neck and arms. She enters a cloister, and after a time an angel releases her from the rings, which eventually decorate her gravestone as a reminder to all.

Though the play is filled with action and lively speeches and contains many allusions to contemporary events, the 16th-century beholder would have had little trouble in perceiving that the people on the stage in front of him were not simply acting out everyday life but presenting a parable on the age-old human themes of guilt and penitence as they struggle within Mariken, who represents man himself in his perilous urge for knowledge. But for us the play is at the same time a cultural myth, one in which life itself is seen in the form of a play. It is not at all accidental that it is while watching a play that Mariken takes the crucial step from guilt to repentance; just as we see ourselves in her acting, she sees herself in the symbolic actors labeled God, Satan and Our Dear Lady. It is a myth primarily because the elaborate stylization of its message according to the rules of the *Rederijkers* itself communicates the underlying meaning of 'play'. Not only is the play written throughout in rhymed couplets – nothing out of the ordinary for the time – but scattered about at many points there occur strophes, sets of lines following a predetermined pattern of rhyme and meter. Each character speaks at least one of these, but the interesting thing is that these highly stylized words are meant as guides to the importance attached to the personalities involved: the Devil has only one, whereas Mariken speaks the largest number of all, and thus indicates her symbolic significance by way of the rhetorical stylization of her language. The most elaborate of her speeches is a famous *refrein* of 32 lines in which, almost precisely at the mid-point of the play, she declaims on Rhetoric itself and its indispensability to life. This innocent piece of self-glorification on the part of the *Rederijkers* seems to be telling us that we live in our language and that the application of *conste*, deliberate refinement, civilizes us and in teaching us to illuminate a thought verbally from all sides enriches our lives. This idea almost seems to be a leaf taken from Erasmus' book.

The *Rederijkers* are expressions of the culture of the Netherlands in still another way. They manifest a strong attachment to the visual that we have already noted in the realm of painting, a trait we will meet many more times. Not only was their typically Medieval organization with its costumes and processions crowded with living allegorical figures a feast for the eye, but they set about satisfying their audiences' hunger for seeing ideas in vivid visual form on the stage, and many painters spent their professional energy working on more and more ingenious stage effects. So thorough was this interaction between ideas and visual representation that it is possible to hold the

Rederijkers at least partially responsible for the development of painting in the Lowlands: figures begin to look more like actors painted from life, and scenes take on the aspect of carefully-executed stage settings.

But cultures are seldom ready for the visionaries they produce, and even though Erasmus represents a vitally important cultural current in the developing bourgeois life in the Renaissance Netherlands, in some ways *Mariken van Nieumeghen* with its idealism but also its anxieties and superstitions gives a more direct reflection of the struggle going on. A society with recognizably modern individualistic traits is coming to be more and more sharply at odds with a cultural organization, the church, modeled on outmoded lines and possessed of a considerable interest in perpetuating its cultural function. Normally we could expect, with Erasmus, that a changing society can modify cultural institutions that have become inappropriate, turning them into a new type of cultural expression. As we have seen, precisely this process was at work in the 16th-century Netherlands, nothing less than a reorienting of the culture's interpretation of man's place in the order of things that evolved in the thought of innovative geniuses like Geert Grote, Desiderius Erasmus and many others. But a very important political reality interfered with what otherwise might have been a quiet evolution. The Netherlands was now dominated by Spain, a culture that was also undergoing change but one in which no comparable reorienting of the religious symbolism was underway; in fact the adherence of this culture to the 'outmoded lines' was expressed in the sincere and determined commitment of the kings of Spain to the continued, unspoiled existence of the faith. The stage was thus set not for the quiet activity of the Brothers of the Common Life but for a much more militant, active response to the challenge. The form the Reformation took in the Netherlands was at first not Lutheran or Calvinist but the appearance of a number of groups that were similar in spirit to the ideals of the Brothers, but that aggressively sought out converts and defied the displeasure of the secular and ecclesiastical authorities. Their preaching against the abuses of the church was of course given extra fuel by the widespread identification of it with a foreign government which was demanding seemingly meaningless taxes. These groups, the most successful of which was probably the Anabaptists, soon brought down on themselves *plakkaten,* decrees restricting or forbidding their activity. The first of a long series of these notorious repressive devices which greatly sharpened already existing discontent was issued in 1536, the very year of Erasmus' death.

6 The ingredients of political liberty

The *plakkaat* of 1536 against religious heretics was issued, as were many other such decrees for a variety of purposes, by Charles' regent in the Netherlands, who at this time was his youthful sister Mary of Hungary. It was for the assistance of Mary, who had just been appointed regent on the sudden death of her aunt Margaret of Savoy, that Charles created in 1530 the Council of State. The regents, personal representatives of the king, had the thankless task of bearing, in their daily high visibility, the whole weight of discontent in an unruly Netherlands they could only partially understand. But they had the incalculable advantage over the king of being on the scene, and therefore much better able to judge what was really happening than the ultimate decision maker in far-off Spain. In this time of increasingly rapid and turbulent change the unfortunate regents have to be given credit for grasping at least that this country was a very different place than Spain and that within limits it had to be allowed to evolve along its own lines, and for constantly trying to convey a true picture of events to Charles.[1] Thus the succession of regents – all but one of them women – placed their modest stamp on the course of events but in the end were powerless to make any real change in its direction. The shaping of the future lay more in the hands of the Council of State, originally conceived as strictly an advisory body.

In 1544 William of Nassau inherited the title Prince of Orange[2] as an eleven year old boy, and although his family was Lutheran – Catholicism and Lutheranism were not yet mutually exclusive – he went to the court at Brussels where he was introduced to court life and educated to his responsibilities to his king, who, as we have already seen, soon made him his favorite. When the Council of State was called into being, its membership was drawn from the noble families already participating in the Habsburg central organization in the Netherlands, families such as Nassau, Egmont and Hoorne. In this way the sons of native Netherlands families were made loyal to the monarchy and trained in ruling the country they knew and understood better than the regents or even the Netherlander Charles V could. In helping to assure continued order and prosperity in the Netherlands, they reflected glory back onto the sovereign under whose (at least theoretically) benign aegis the state existed and whose legitimacy nobody questioned. Though they were all from staunchly Catholic families, they knew that the disturbing religious unrest in the Netherlands was not the irresponsible work of a few wild-eyed fanatics, as it appeared to his Catholic Majesty, but a clear articulation of a widespread political unrest. They, even more than the regents, found themselves caught in the middle between the political stake of their rightful sovereign and the by now noticeably different political interests of the Netherlands people. They tried to carry on their mediating function as long as they could, representing a collection of age-old 'privileges' to a monarch who had the job of holding together a large and unwieldy empire, and did this with fair success as long as Charles remained the head of the state. But when later their sovereign, whom they had been brought up to recognize as the keystone of the whole state structure and the guarantor of all its liberties, failed to comprehend them and even disclaimed any responsibility for them, they were thrown into an intolerable crisis of conscience and forced to choose between a hallowed ideal and the person occupying the throne. When they became convinced that the king had renounced his claim to represent their national interests, their choice was made. The one most agonized by these developments was William of Nassau, a Catholic prince from a German Lutheran family who had the genius to perceive before anyone else did that Netherlands society was in the process of creating new cultural forms that were uniquely suited to it, and that this must be allowed to proceed. It is one of the typical ironies of history, though, that its actors are usually unaware of the true significance of what they are doing; as we will see presently, William of Nassau thought to the end that he was fighting to preserve the old order.

Though the causes of historical events are complex and reach far back in time, it is still possible to point to one event that created a deep split between the people of the Netherlands and their ruler and made revolt inevitable: the accession of Philip II to the Spanish throne in 1555. In 1543 his father Charles V united the seventeen Netherlands provinces into a single unit and formally separated them from the German empire, so that his son, who would not automatically be elected emperor of Germany, could nevertheless inherit the Netherlands along with Spain. In his not unreasonable treatment of the Netherlands as a province of Spain, Philip unwittingly provided the challenge to which the culture of the Netherlands was to respond with its most significant display of creative energy. It was now – as our long perspective can show us – as ready for the challenge as it ever would be, having built up a strong tradition on the old Medieval concept of 'privilege' that by now had evolved stable forms that shaped a whole society. When we pause to take stock a little further along we will note again the curious fact that these stabilized forms are at one and the same time the old way everybody struggles to defend and the new order on which ultimately the Republic is founded. In 1555 we find ourselves confronted with a clear political polarization that coincides with a religious one. The point to keep close watch on from now on is how the religious reorientation we have talked about departs from the contemplative realm and turns into the expression of reaction and – characteristic of the Netherlands, at the same time – the banner of political change.[3]

In 1555 Spain, and therefore also the Netherlands, was embroiled in a war with France. During the next four years Philip spent most of his time in the Netherlands, where encounters with the French were

73

taking place and where large numbers of Spanish troops were station-ed. It was not by any means a Spanish operation on Northern soil; Philip was heavily dependent on both the financial resources and the political and military leadership of the Netherlands to carry on the war. When peace negotiations finally took place, William of Nassau (or William of Orange, as he was now more commonly called) was one of those sent as personal representatives of the king. Before Philip left the Netherlands in 1559, never to return, he did several things. His sister Margaret of Parma was made regent of the Netherlands, several important nobles were rewarded for their faithful service with the title *stadhouder* (one which from now on we will treat as English and not bother to italicize), among them Egmont, Hoorne, and William of Orange – the latter becoming stadhouder of Holland, Zeeland and Utrecht –, and these and others became members of the Council of State to govern jointly with Margaret. A much less welcome honor came to William of Orange and to Hoorne when they were made commanders of the Spanish troops that remained in the Netherlands to protect the southern borders from the French. Under the surface, however, relations were strained. Philip left the Netherlands alarmed by the extent of what he interpreted as religious heresy and was determined to suppress it by the same means he was using in Spain, the Inquisition. He was also resentful of the unexpected independence of the Netherlands nobility and the representatives in the States General whom he addressed just prior to his departure; particularly the former had an infuriating way of neglecting to defer to the fact that he was the absolute ruler of a powerful, centralized modern state, and treating him in the old Medieval fashion as merely the first among sovereign equals – and of course he was right. The Netherlands still clung to an archaic social order and had never developed a central authority along Renaissance lines, the kind that in the rest of Europe was visibly reflected in the prestigious monarchies.

Though Philip was repeatedly reminded by those witnessing events in the Netherlands that political unity could not possibly be achieved by increasingly sterner religious repression, he could see conditions only from the Spanish point of view. A new wave of unrest resulted when the number of Catholic bishops in the Netherlands was increased from four to eighteen, something looked on with distaste not only by the tiny Protestant minority but also by the Catholic majority who interpreted it as Spanish interference. Resentment turned on Cardinal Granvelle, who had accumulated considerable power in the Netherlands and was ruling without consulting the Council of State. At the same time the predictably unwelcome Spanish troops were running wild and terrorizing the population they were originally assigned to protect. Protests from the Netherlands nobility did some good: in 1561 3000 troops were sent home, and in 1564, following a letter to the king, Granvelle was recalled. By this time Calvinism, a new form of Protestantism brought in from Switzerland, had entered the scene and was having considerable success in spite of all attempts to suppress it. These attempts, carrying out the king's wishes expressed in the form of *plakkaten,* were so obviously achieving the opposite of the result intended that Egmont went personally to Spain with a petition to the king. When this was ignored, a group of the lower nobility whose hands were not tied by being personal representatives of the king went to Margaret with a plea for a more flexible policy. The issue of religious liberty was more and more becoming identified with the political interests of large segments of the population, and a religious split inevitably meant a political split. Though Margaret had considerable sympathy for the aspirations she witnessed in Netherlands society, she was alarmed at the increasing disorder; she transmitted the petition of this group (which a courtier referred to as *gueux,* beggars, a name which thereafter was adopted with pride by the whole revolt movement in the Dutch form *geuzen* and used many times since then, most recently as the name of an early resistance group in World War II) to the king, who rejected it as well. This was in 1566; the result, in the same year, was the *Beeldenstorm,* a furious iconoclastic outburst that destroyed Catholic religious symbols in churches throughout the Netherlands.

With this the polarization had reached a point from which it could no longer turn back. We should notice carefully that the violence that now becomes more and more common does not remind us at all of a revolution, but much more of a civil war. The Protestants, including those who use the badge of Protestantism as a cover for other interests, turn their anger on the Catholic part of the population who happen also to be theoretically loyal to the Spanish king; the Catholics, in turn, regard the Protestants as fanatic troublemakers who are hand in glove with the arrogant patricians of the cities. And it was not only a clash of social blocs but also of regions: Holland and Zeeland, dominated by the rich city merchants for centuries now, were breeding places for Calvinism and other forms of religious particularism, whereas Gelderland and Overijsel to the East were dominated by the landed gentry who remained attached to Catholicism; Flanders to the South, traditionally an arena of social conflict, was now itself polarized confessionally along the old political lines of urban population versus aristocracy. Over the entire Netherlands it is now the Protestants — whether they are specifically Calvinist or not — who hold the political initiative in their hands and begin to turn a wide variety of social and political interests into a coherent action. This action is led precisely by those provinces having the heaviest concentration of Protestants, Flanders and Brabant in the South and Holland in the North.

Philip's answer to the *Beeldenstorm* was to send 10,000 troops to the Netherlands under the command of the Duke of Alba, the act that brought on a crisis for the Netherlands nobles. Egmond and Hoorne renewed their oath of allegiance and hoped to soften Alba's vengeance as much as possible, but William of Orange refused, although he was not yet ready to throw in his lot with the militant Protestants; as a loyal Catholic prince he had in fact recently denied a band of aggressive *geuzen* sanctuary in Antwerp and thus ensured their destruction. He now resigned his post as stadhouder and fled to his family's castle in Germany where he considered his next move. It was at about this time or during the setbacks that were to follow that a song was written about him that has since become the national anthem of the Netherlands. The first two lines — usually still written today in the original 16th century spelling — are

> Wilhelmus van Nassouwen
> ben ick van Duytschen bloedt.

and the last two lines of the first verse:

> Den koninck van Hispaengien
> heb ick altijt gheeert.*

He firmly believed that if he were to take the step of open rebellion he would actually be fighting for the king against those who had grossly deceived him about the true picture in the Netherlands. Pressure was put on him to lead the cause of revolt, and when he became convinced of the extent of the support he could depend on from those whose interests previously ran counter to his — for instance, both the heavily protestant city patricians in Holland and the Calvinist lower classes now clamoring for tax relief — he chose the side of the *geuzen*. In 1568 Egmont and Hoorne were treacherously arrested and beheaded on the marketplace in Brussels, and in the same year William invaded the Netherlands as the Eighty Years' War began.

The events of the first few years were nothing but a series of defeats, and William's support was far weaker than he had hoped in spite of Alba's increasingly stern repressive measures. When he was forced to withdraw back to Germany from the field of action in the eastern provinces, resistance forces in the West continued to rally support for the revolt and began actively harassing Spanish shipping off the coast. The first turning point in the struggle came in 1572 when a group of these latter captured and occupied a coastal town and set off an uprising all over the country. Protestant forces had been quietly growing in strength, and now within a few months nearly all the larger towns came under their control. At this point there was a clear national cause, and the Calvinist form of Protestantism became thoroughly identified with it. The spread of Calvinism throughout the land was not a matter of some predisposition in the Dutch people, as has

*William of Nassau / I am, of German blood. / The King of Spain / I have always honored.

77

often been claimed, but more a matter of political realities. The confession was spread partly by force and even violence, because profession of it came to be an indispensible gauge of political loyalty. At some point in the early 1570's William of Orange too became Protestant, not because theology particularly interested him but simply because it reflected the change in his political loyalty. Soon after the uprising a group of cities declared him their stadhouder, whereupon − not without hesitation at accepting the leadership of so many different interests − he disbanded his German troops and came to Holland.

In the next years of war William struggled to break the Spanish siege on many of the rebellious cities and wrest more territory from Spanish control, all the while maintaining an uneasy alliance with the undisciplined troops he commanded. A destructive outbreak of mutiny among the Spanish troops so alarmed the Netherlands population that it resulted in 1576 in a first loose confederation of the Netherlands provinces, the Pacification of Gent, by which they determined to rid the country of all Spanish troops and give formal recognition to the Reformation . . . in Holland and Zeeland, but nowhere else. This united front did in fact result in the recall of the Spanish troops, and in 1577 William made a triumphal entry into Brussels. But it was not strong enough to withstand the inevitable reaction from the Spanish side to what seemed an attempt on the part of the Netherlands provinces to go entirely their own way, and soon there were again Spanish troops in the South. William sought help from the French against Spain, but the St. Bartholomew massacre of Protestants in 1572 was still fresh in memory, and he lost considerable Protestant support, especially in the South. But the continued movement toward unity of action led to a new agreement in 1579, the Union of Utrecht. This significant treaty bound the seven northern provinces together and guaranteed freedom of religion, and is still the basis of the modern Netherlands state. Two weeks later the southern provinces ratified their own Union of Arras, making peace with the king of Spain. The separation of one state into two was now a fact, and from now on we can begin speaking of the development of two societies and two cultures.

At the time the document establishing the Union of Utrecht was drawn up, William of Orange was in Brussels trying to salvage what he could of his primary vision, the union of both North and South in a sovereign state. When he returned to Holland and added his signature four months later, it was with a feeling that he had failed and not that he had helped create a new state. His attempt to offer the sovereignty of the northern provinces to the French Anjous made him many enemies, and his loose alliance with the Protestant merchants and the militant rebels came to pieces rapidly. The Spanish overestimated his popularity and put a price on his head, thinking that if he should be removed from the scene the whole northern union would fall apart. But he had provided better leadership than he thought, and when he was assassinated in 1584 in Delft the Netherlands provinces had already begun growing beyond him into a new era. Though he had shown uncommon flexibility in abandoning the prejudices of a feudal prince and assuming the moral leadership of a ragged collection of jealous sovereign provinces, he could not suspect that the political and religious wrangling he witnessed on all sides could ever lead to meaningful unity. And yet, although by far the most bitter internal struggles were still to come, this is just what happened.

The question of William's political creativity and independence at a crucial period in history versus the force exerted on events by much wider tendencies has naturally been extensively debated.[4] The most reasonable point of view seems to be that while his development from the ruler of an obscure principality to someone rightfully looked on as the 'father of his country' shows a singular ability to give form and direction to events, his career has to be seen in the context of powerful forces that were working in a parallel direction. Foremost of these was the continuing evolution of the merchant aristocracy that already had a strong grip on the culture of the Netherlands, that was giving its cities the architectural face that has been their pride ever since and that was trading in the far corners of the world. This explosive commercial expansion in the North could not remain forever tied to the economy of Spain, and the ultimate independence of the North seems even more inevitable from the military point of view because of the natural barrier formed by the great rivers that separate North and South. William's role might reasonably be thought of as a focusing of all these interests that was courageous and insightful but also to a great extent symbolic.

The new form the union of the Seven Provinces was taking is scarcely perceptible yet at this point. They were left without a leader and had wide freedom of choice for a replacement, but in the 16th century a state without a visible monarch was such an unheard-of anomaly that it occurred to nobody to simply govern by some type of ruling council with an elected head; or perhaps it would be more accurate to say that although the city aristocrats who dominated the States General would have been happy to attempt this, they knew that the popular forces arrayed against them would not have permitted it. Accordingly the sovereignty was offered again to the French, and then to the English Earl of Leicester, an important member of Queen Elizabeth's court. Leicester arrived in 1585, knowing little about the problems peculiar to the Netherlands provinces, and in 1587 left again in disgrace and frustration. He had been unprepared, just as Philip II and all his representatives had been, for the confident assumption on the part of the merchants that they had a right to a strong voice in government and for the economic leverage they could mobilize to back up their demands. Leicester had the added misfortune to collide with the most forceful leader this class had ever yet had, Johan van Oldenbarnevelt, who held a key position in the government of the province of Holland. Oldenbarnevelt had developed an office of relative insignificance into a base for far-reaching power, so much that he was able to see to it that Prince Maurits, the son of William of Orange, was appointed — over Leicester's head — stadhouder of Holland and Zeeland, general of the armed forces and admiral of the fleet.

The year 1588 is a historical milestone because it saw the spectacular defeat of the Spanish Armada sent against England, a blow from which Spain never really recovered. For our own study this year is equally important because it was only now, thanks partly to the confidence provided by the disaster the Spanish suffered, that the Netherlands provinces began going their own way without a monarch. The famous ten-year span from 1588 to 1598, the year in which Philip II of Spain died, witnessed the transformation of the Netherlands provinces from a shaky and demoralized confederation of clashing interests into a unified state ready to take its place alongside the other European powers. The responsibilities of government were shared jointly by Prince Maurits and Oldenbarnevelt, at first sight a very unlikely team. Maurits was a noble and a soldier who had very little interest in the fine points of politics; the luster of the Orange name gave him a great deal of support among the common people who had suffered most from the heavy hand of the Spanish and who were strongly Calvinist, especially in Holland. Oldenbarnevelt was a liberal Protestant from the class that around this time comes to be called the 'Regents', the culturally dominant class to whom the entire next chapter will be devoted. He was a consummate politician and organizer who helped establish once and for all the economic, political and cultural predominance of Holland over all the other provinces. The Regents had strong misgivings about this alliance, since they were suspicious of the military and felt little kinship with the lower classes who formed their moral support. In return, these same classes nourished a profound dislike for the wealthy, arrogant Regents who attempted to rule according to their own special interests. But this alliance was held together by the desperate necessity to resist the Spanish, who still held large sections of the Netherlands under their military control. By the end of ten years they had succeeded in uniting the country under a central authority and providing the means for driving back the Spanish until they showed an unmistakable desire to end hostilities, but it is fairly clear that in fact they succeeded a bit too well: Maurits' highly visible military successes made him so popular that the Regents developed a long-standing suspicion that a

81

powerful noble family could have monarchic ambitions, and Olden-barnevelt's single-minded determination to consolidate political power in the hands of a few influential rulers in Holland created a whole array of enemies he sadly underestimated.

By 1609 the war had become sufficiently stalemated that a cease-fire was agreed upon, the Twelve-Year Truce the very signing of which by the Spanish implied recognition of the sovereignty of the Netherlands. It was at this point, when the immediate danger was removed, that the political struggle going on in the country burst out into the open. The form it took was that of a religious quarrel. As we have already noted, the rigidly intolerant, militant form of orthodox 16th century Cal-vinism was well adapted – came to be adapted – to the harsh political realities of the time. Thus a specific theological position came to be identified with the political interests of a particular class, in spite of this class' utter ignorance of theology of any kind. It should not be surprising if in this kind of climate radically different political inter-ests come to be identified with opposing theological positions, and this is just what happened. By a route that we will consider in more detail later on, the Regents found themselves best served by a more flexible and liberal position that had been formed by people like Geert Grote and Erasmus. It is not that they were particularly liberal-ly-minded people – their politics tend rather to betray quite the opposite cast of mind – but more that they made common cause with a theological position that was at least not incompatible with their prejudices and ambitions.

Just prior to the Truce an academic dispute had arisen between Franciscus Gomarus, representing the 'right', and Jacobus Arminius, representing the 'left', on the interpretation of some doctrinal points in a narrow or broad sense. The place of religion in the culture's sytem of values is immediately apparent in the fact that this dispute was in reality the articulation of the deep national split into *preciezen*, those who insisted on doctrinal purity, and *rekkelijken*, those who were willing to allow latitude in interpretation. Particularly the latter felt themselves disadvantaged in their freedom of worship, and in 1610 issued a Remonstrance setting forth their views. When this was followed the next year by their opponents' Counter-remonstrance, the polarization was complete and the fight was on. Matters reached a crisis stage when by around 1618 the polarization had reached the national leadership itself and split the country irrevocably: Maurits was interested chiefly in military matters but found himself defending the rights of the orthodox Gomarists, while Oldenbarnevelt vigorously championed the cause of the liberal Arminians. The result was a national synod, the Synod of Dordrecht, called in 1618, which ended in 1619 in victory for the Gomarists. Though the theological outcome was relatively insignificant since by this time both religious outlooks had evolved a modus vivendi which permitted both to coexist in grudging acceptance, the political outcome was a tragic one. Oldenbarnevelt's independence had carried him a step too far, and the state reacted to the danger of arbitrary control by executing one of its foremost founders in The Hague in 1619, at the age of 72 years.[5]

In 1621 the Truce ended and the war with Spain was resumed, with more of a sense of obligation than enthusiasm on both sides. By this time Spain's fortunes were declining sharply and Europe was becoming increasingly engulfed in the disastrous Thirty Years' War. With England now the chief rival, the future of the United Provinces seemed assured. The national unification of factions begun by William of Orange and brought to maturity by Maurits and Oldenbarnevelt was showing unmistakable signs of viability – no small claim in the fiercely competitive world of 17th-century Europe.

7 The anatomy of a Golden Age

Cultural history presents few challenges quite equal that of attempting to bring together the multitude of social and economic factors necessary to explain how a culture produces the harmonious flowering of civilization that can be called its 'Golden Age'. Most cultures seem to have known a period in which in some remarkable way the 'rules of the game' worked so perfectly and took on such far-reaching implications that they stimulated a concerted creativity on all sides. In the case of the Netherlands during the early years of the Republic – in round figures, roughly from 1600 to 1650 – the inherent fascination of this challenge is heightened by the fact that this Golden Age came about in an extremely small area, and made unique by the apparently unprecedented fact that it burst onto the scene almost immediately upon the birth of the state itself. Huizinga begins his classic study of this period *Nederland's beschaving in de zeventiende eeuw*[1] by raising precisely this question, and then proceeds to focus on the spirit of the seventeenth-century cultural achievements by the simple but effective device of beginning with the most obvious physical circumstances and progressively narrowing down his field of vision onto the heart of its inspiration: the nature of the chief creators of this culture. We can most profitably follow this same line of attack on the subject, not trying to cover all the same ground but instead keeping in view all the ground we have covered up to this point and constantly asking, as we consider a variety of cultural expressions, what kind of cultural 'game' will account for what we can observe. It is thus not so much the familiar cultural expressions we are interested in as it is the people who produced them. In this chapter we will look more closely at the underlying social structure' and some of the circumstances that gave it its form, and the two following chapters will be devoted to a few of the ways this society expressed its innermost form in the creation of a new symbolic system out of an old one.

We are interested most intensely in this very continuity with the past. the ways in which the culture constantly gives new form to old symbols, but a survey of the array of Netherlands provinces that emerged in the Union of Utrecht immediately makes clear that their participation in this past was uneven indeed. Most of the heartland of Burgundian culture now lay in Spanish-held territory, a break in tradition that even the considerable waves of immigration to the North had not been able to change. Of the seven northern provinces themselves, Groningen, Overijsel and Gelderland to the north and east were conservative areas that remained dominated by the old nobility; Friesland was brought close by family connections in the House of Orange but otherwise remained a somewhat distant outpost; Utrecht was close to the geographical center of the union but lacked economic independence, possibly as a result of the centuries-long administration by ecclesiastical authorities; Zeeland in the extreme west was progressive but ever since the 13th century had been dominated by either the South or the North. Even less need be said about the *generaliteits- landen,* occupied territories in the South that were run by the provinces but had no say in its policies and no hope for economic development.

This leaves only Holland, the real nerve center of the union from which, as Huizinga remarks, the rest must have had the appearance of an extremely fragile but colorful fabric. Holland had participated fully in the Burgundian culture, less glamorously than Flanders and Brabant in the South perhaps, but absorbing and integrating its gain in its own way. We can return now to a point we made quite some time back: Holland developed economically and politically somewhat later than some of the other Medieval states, but this delay allowed it to emerge dominant onto a scene with far greater potential for cultural creativity. The cities of Holland were still at their economic peak in the 16th century, the period in which the tradition of 'privilege' had gotten so thoroughly integrated into economic and political life that a concerted effort could be aroused in response to the challenge offered by Spanish rule. It was, in other words, the particular social form evolved in Holland from the feudal past, plus its solidly-based economic prosperity, that supported the vision of William of Orange and that was transformed into an independent force by the genius of Johan van Oldenbarnevelt. Taking up another strand we dropped several chapters back, it is possible to see that the very physical challenge imposed by the geographical area Holland occupied required a response of unique proportions. The vast system of dikes and waterways necessary to make the land habitable and enable the circulation of goods within it required such elaborate care that the development of a high level of coordination of effort was almost inevitable. It is not at all irresponsible to claim that this very practical need for local initiative and cooperation of equals was a stronger force working in the direction of creating a democratic frame of mind than commercial competition or the Burgundian ideal of a centralized harmony. The ever-present wind, easily exploitable and available to all, is another not negligible factor, although economically it may be less striking a factor than Holland's valuable proximity to the sea.

Shipping became more and more the single commercial activity on which the economy rested, one which had reached such a level of growth that during the Eighty Years' War the Dutch even managed to make the Spanish dependent on them and so obtain a strong hold on their economy. The best situated port was Amsterdam, a relatively late arrival in the community of cities but one which now underwent its period of sudden expansion just in time to assume the economic and political leadership of the entire province. It absorbed large numbers of Jews fleeing from the Inquisition in Spain and Portugal, and even larger numbers of Protestants who were forced to

leave southern cities such as Antwerp when they passed into permanent Spanish control. Economic and political leadership, coupled
with worldwide interests and a large infusion of peoples from elsewhere, ensures cultural leadership as well, and this is where the focus
of our interest will be.

The fall of Antwerp to the Spanish in 1585, of great cultural importance because it resulted in the migration northward of many prominent citizens, was also of great economic importance because it left
the mouth of the Schelde firmly in the military control of the
Zeelanders who had been helping to defend the city. It was hence-
forth closed to all shipping, and there is probably no more striking
example of the crassly opportunistic aspects of the concept of 'privilege' than in the way this advantage was pressed to its limit: in the
Truce of 1609 the right of the United Provinces to keep the Schelde
closed to shipping was explicitly recognized, and even in the final
peace treaty with Spain in 1648 this now superfluous right was
insisted on as inalienable. Whatever the moral judgement may be, the
result was naturally the complete collapse of the prosperity of
Antwerp, the foremost port of the South, and the corresponding rise
of the role of Amsterdam. The story of the commercial activity of
Amsterdam in the early 17th century is too well known to need
summary here; in a word, the Dutch now opened up a trade territory
of almost unlimited scope, relying very little on domestic products
and very heavily on the middleman role of carrying cargo for others.
They were so successful in getting a grip on the economies of their
neighbors that they were widely hated and feared, but also grudgingly
admired: everyone asked how they were able to do it.

One factor that was easily noticed was that the Dutch had somehow
managed to put new vigor into an archaic, pre-mercantilistic economic
system. Where in France, Spain and England a strong central authority
was able to impose order and uniformity on the state functions and
guide its economy, in the Netherlands no such central authority had
ever come into being, and the economy, over which the central States

87

General had no control, was still a 'privilege'-based hodgepodge of different forms of competition that unavoidably made individual enterprise a valuable asset. And yet this early free-enterprise system should not be thought of too idealistically as a noble experiment in freedom and democracy, an interpretation which would ignore its ruthless aspects just as no interpretation of religious developments in 16th and 17th century society would be complete that did not take account of the prevalence of savage intolerance. Nevertheless, it remains true that whereas in other countries Medieval particularism had to be done away with by force in order to assure the step into modern times, in the Netherlands this old particularism in the realms of economy, politics and religion (actually all aspects of the same thing, as we have been seeing) was controlled and transformed just in time to become a positive pattern in the culture that stoutly resisted all attempts to change it. Thus in their determined fight to preserve the old order, William of Orange and Maurits on the one side and Oldenbarnevelt and the city Regents on the other were in reality presiding over the birth of a new system that simply skipped over the era of absolute centralization and mercantilism and rested on the 'pillars' – to reintroduce our pun – of individualism. It is now time to narrow down our focus once more to consider the society of people who created this disorderly but vigorous style of doing things. Were they people who had the courage and vision to dare to be independent, or were they too shortsighted and stubborn to look beyond their own immediate interests?

The class we have been variously calling, ever since the heart of the Middle Ages, the wealthy merchants, city aristocrats, Regents and the like has been steadily growing and assuming an importance in increasingly wider areas. At a very early time this class begins filling the power vacuum left by the decline of the ecclesiastical hierarchy – never really strong in the Netherlands to begin with – and the withering away of the nobility. There is abundant evidence that by the 14th century there is a highly-developed urban cultural consciousness that is able to breed the distinctly 'modern', sophisticated thought of people like Geert Grote and Erasmus. Their cultural identification was so well-articulated by the 16th century that they were able to muster wide support for the resistance to outside incursions into their established ways. In 17th-century Amsterdam this prosperous class had established many of the same social habits we see plainly in 14th-century Deventer or even in 13th-century Bruges, but habits that were peculiarly well adapted to the realities of urban life. They were, if anything, intensely practical businessmen who saw that their valuable contacts with all kinds of people could only be successfully carried on by treating business as business and treating niceties such as religion, politics or regional origin as not particularly relevant to everyday social interaction. They thus deliberately cultivated a new type of urbane politeness, a social game that was played by the rules of acceptance, tolerance, self-control and reserve. Nobody pretended that tolerance had to run very deep: you were free to think as you liked about others' misguided ways but you kept your sentiments to yourself. It was at about this time that a clear distinction evolved in the language, as it did in all the other European vernaculars, between intimate and polite forms of address. The pronoun *gij* came to be used, like older English *ye* and French *vous*, for polite address, while a related form *jij* assumed, like English *thou* and French *tu*, the role of informal or intimate address. In the development of this polite reserve we witness a form of interaction between people which is a blend of Burgundian polish and the practicality of urban Holland, and which was so successful a cultural structuring of social life that centuries later it was still drawing more and more levels of Netherlands society toward it. Here the habit of accepting other groups as equals that began in the crude necessities of 'privilege' has been formalized and integrated on the strictly individual level to become the innermost rules of the cultural game itself. These rules are those of a middle-class society that does, to be sure, value a certain ostentation expressed in the fine houses it builds with classical motifs on the narrow façades, but that at the same time remains very insistent on a general sober morality. Worldwide business contacts are not incompatible with a small-town interest in the extent to which one's neighbors observe the accepted standards of propriety. This matter-of-fact preoccupation with the everyday, which is inherited from the Middle Ages and which we will have a great deal more to say about in a later chapter, is no doubt the reason why Holland seems to have remained largely immune to the flamboyant Baroque style that overwhelmed the taste of the other 17th-century European cultures.

We can not have an adequate understanding of what held this style of life together before we have tried to understand one or two deeper aspects of its *levensbeschouwing*. It is one of the more remarkable facts about the cultural history of the Netherlands that a class we have every right to expect to be outstandingly orthodox and conservative in its confessional persuasions nevertheless turns out to be the prime champion of a remarkable liberalism that it carries with it in its progress toward cultural dominance. While it is an obvious over-simplification to talk about only two religious outlooks, orthodox and liberal, in the midst of a host of different religious points of view, the fact is that there was a constant tendency for these many groups to make common cause and polarize into two opposing camps, partic- ularly when, as at the time of the Synod of Dordrecht, these followed a political polarization. For a variety of reasons the Regent class found itself in alliance with the tolerant, liberal bloc, not only because of political realities but because this point of view best articulated its own cultural persuasions – not surprisingly in view of the fact that this culture had provided the soil on which the liberal thought flourished. Its first two prophets were both Catholics, and the next link in the chain was provided by still another Catholic, Dirck Volkertszoon Coornhert.

Coornhert, whose brooding, white-bearded face gazes out at us in the painting by Cornelisz, was a copper engraver, painter and writer who was active in the political affairs of Holland and served for a time as an official in its government. He wrote his *Zedekunst, dat is wellevenskunste*[2] in 1586, the year in which Oldenbarnevelt came to power. The *Zedekunst* is an attempt to formulate an ethical philosophy that could serve as a reasoned guide to practical, everyday living, an early example of the kind of work that was to reach great heights of popularity in the Rationalistic 17th and 18th centuries. It is not Catholic in any sense, but betrays throughout the pragmatic, tolerant humanism of urban Holland. The point is to show how man can live the most fruitful, virtuous life under the guidance of reason. Man is born with life, but not the 'right' life (the *welleven* of his title), which it is the prime task of man to develop. This right life is a potentiality that resides in each man, the nurturing of which requires instruction and practice. Coornhert is a product of the 16th century, not the 18th, and so he holds resolutely to the idea that although man is not burdened by original sin, he can never really attain the 'right' stage by himself but requires God as a teacher. At times he sounds distinctly Medieval: everyday knowledge is the lower knowledge of images, but there is a higher, direct knowledge of eternal realities these images and reflections point to. But the difference is that Coornhert turns the relation around and makes man's inner experience the decisive point and not the top of the hierarchy of knowledge. It is through human existence that the eternal things are known, and rightness can be verified only by inner experience. Coornhert is suspicious of everything that tends to take responsibility out of the individual's own will-directed searching, especially institutions such as dogma, confession, the sacraments, the idea of predestination, in fact the church itself with all its claim to authority. Each man is individually perfectible but must find the way himself by exercising his own grasp of truth as he finds it in his own experience, and there is no way of imposing any single standard on everyone. It is apparent that this striking emphasis on individual experience and insistence on freedom from centralized authority in a *levensbeschouwing* that is in a peculiar resonance with some of the most cherished values of the culture of Holland still evolving in this time. So strongly does it reflect the persuasions of the Regent culture that it puts the individual's religious 'privilege' ahead of the claims of either Catholic or Protestant thought.

Naturally Coornhert made himself many enemies in all parts of the confessional spectrum. He died in 1590, and never witnessed the most dramatic vindication of his work. No less a theologian than Jacobus Arminius was assigned the task of refuting Coornhert's heresy, but when he immersed himself in his writings he found himself becoming convinced that it was Coornhert who was right. Arminius became the spokesman of the whole liberal movement and eventually, as we saw, confronted the orthodox Gomarus over the issue of religious flexibility versus strictness. By this he became the father of the Remonstrants, a small group that today is still to be found near the liberal end of the confessional spectrum in the Netherlands.[3] In the early 17th century religious liberalism was the shibboleth of the Regent class, and Calvinistic orthodoxy that of its counterbalancing political force, the Prince and his power base in the more humble classes; when in 1619 the Synod of Dordrecht placed its seal of approval on the latter, it was indulging in a political act that represented a setback for the oligarchic Regents but that on a different level encouraged a marked cultural tendency toward the sober and puritanical.

And yet the Synod in another sense did not really speak with the voice of the future. Even as it ensured a conservative triumph, the stream of tolerant liberalism had so thoroughly permeated the dominant culture, puritanical as it was in many ways, that it became a bit difficult to single out just what was supposed to be suppressed. Though Coornhert himself made no attempt to attract followers, through the instrumentality of Arminius and with the cultural prestige of the cultivated middle class, his thought gradually joined that of Erasmus and Geert Grote in a blend of conservatism and liberalism that was a peculiarly faithful articulation of the underlying nature of not only the ruling classes but increasingly wider segments of the society. It was largely this that created the unique climate in which Descartes, Spinoza – who spent three years with the Coornhert-inspired Rijnsburg Collegiants – and Locke, to mention only three, could find a hospitable sanctuary from intolerance.

92

The culture that suddenly burst into prominence at the end of the 16th century and the beginning of the 17th is not, after all, one that ought to astound us overly much by its appearing immediately upon the emergence of the newly independent state, especially when we are aware of the extent of its debt to previous stages. Its continuity and its genius is precisely its determined yet flexible hold on the past, resulting in its ability to maintain much of the old 'game' with only minor adjustments of the rules. In spite of an undeniable air of noblesse oblige about the culture of the 17th century, its moralistic preoccupation with practical rightness and its reverence for the everyday never fail to betray the humbler origins it tenaciously clung to. The earliest clear evidence of the internal health and balance of this culture that was able to blur the sharp distinctions between noble and common and between ecclesiastical and secular comes in its reflection of itself in architecture. Its creation of the Holland Renaissance in the late years of the 16th century and the early years of the 17th, which built wealthy houses, churches and public buildings throughout the Netherlands and in all the neighboring countries, shows in its harmony of form and function a level of taste that leaves no room for doubt that a genuinely classical 'Golden Age' is under way.

By at least 1600 the Republic had come into being and was firmly established, in fact if not yet in name. It is an anomaly in the family of nations, something that should not really be at all, and has no accepted designation other than the Seven Provinces, the United Provinces, the States General, or similar terms. It is only when, after many more years of war, the treaties that end both the Eighty Years' War and the Thirty Years' War are signed in 1648 in Münster in Westphalia that the existence of the Dutch Republic is officially recognized. Its cultural flourishing all came within a very short period, beginning somewhere around the turn of the century and by 1648 already showing unmistakable signs of rigidity and fatigue. In *The Dutch Republic,* a book which to an admirable extent succeeds in presenting the whole panorama of life in this period, Wilson attempts to capture its remarkable spirit with the words 'the rebel provinces comprised, then, a *pays sans frontières.* The seeds of tolerance and freedom that had been latent through the Burgundian era of noble, ecclesiastical and municipal privileges and 'liberties' now burgeoned with fresh vigour.'[4] The mere task of keeping track of our 'rules of the game' in a culture assuming international dimensions will not be an easy one.

8 A manner of speaking

With considerable justification, the texts in which we can find the story of 17th-century culture largely ignore the other six provinces and concentrate on Holland, the one that provided over half the total budget, and narrow down their scope even within these few square miles to the one city that with its worldwide commercial and intellectual ferment dominated all the rest. There is banking on an international scale, trade and colonization as far as the influence of the East India Company extends, shipbuilding and exploring; Hugo de Groot, an Arminian liberal who was arrested in 1619 along with Oldenbarnevelt but escaped from prison and went into temporary exile, now writes epoch-making works on international law; the brilliant mathematician and engineer Simon Stevin had been called to the University of Leiden on its founding by William of Orange on the lifting of the Spanish siege in 1575 and extended his interests over a wide variety of scientific fields, insisting on the Renaissance's objective how rather than the Middle Ages' theological why; such diverse fields as cartography, anatomy, navigation and optics bring international recognition to investigators like Huygens and Leeuwenhoek, who combine unexcelled observational skill with practical usefulness. But important as these achievements are for an understanding of the totality of 17th-century culture in the Netherlands, they are after all part of a cultural picture that is actually continental in scope and contributed to in no small measure by countries with much different social structures such as England, France, Spain and now also Denmark and Sweden. If we are to continue successfully our search for the social game underlying observable cultural manifestations and generating them, we will do best to choose an aspect of the culture whose limitation to this culture and only this one cannot be seriously questioned. Since our discussion makes no attempt to substitute for readings in cultural history but only to bring them together into a coherent picture, we can safely afford to depart rather radically now from the usual picture given.

Surely the most inalienable possession of a culture is its language. It is not quite enough just to say that the culture of the Dutch Republic has as its instrument of communication the Dutch language (whatever might be meant by that); every culture without exception requires a language for its transmission, and since anything that can be said in one language can be said in any other, even though perhaps a bit clumsily, in theory any language could have served equally well for the transmission of the culture of the Netherlands and for communication within the society. What in fact happens is that a culture is continually laying down its rules in the language itself, making it into an absolutely unique and unsubstitutable cultural manifestation. In other words, the language of one culture will not do for the transmission of another culture after all because it goes far beyond answering the need for social interaction pure and simple and reflects the culture's peculiar way of structuring these interactions. The speaking of a language accordingly takes on many aspects of playing by the rules of the cultural 'game', which means that study of certain aspects of the life of the language can be extremely revealing of some aspects of this game. All this, again, is true of any culture; in dealing with an advanced literate culture we have a far more fertile field at our disposal in that we might find out what happens when members of the culture get to saying things not only *in* their language but also *about* it.

Through most of the Middle Ages a person's context of social interaction went little beyond his village, at most the little duchy in which he lived, and his language reflected this situation faithfully: it was very much like that of the next village and yet had at least a few distinct peculiarities of its own. Such gradually differing forms of speech are better called dialects than languages because their mutual intelligibility gives their speakers some awareness that they are speaking variant forms of the same generalized language. These variant dialects gradually differing from village to village and from duchy to principality to bishopric spread without clear borders from the northern boundary of where French was spoken throughout the Lowlands and across northern Germany. These dialect forms of speech are exceedingly conservative, being the result of long occupation of a particular area by a cohesive social group, but they are nevertheless constantly in a state of slow change. Change takes place when certain words or pronunciations of one dialect begin to be imitated by its neighbors, and the most evident reason why this should happen is that this imitated dialect is spoken in an area that has become politically or culturally dominant over its neighbors. A study of the picture of the dialects spoken today thus gives us a sort of frozen display of cultural happenings in the past which, studied carefully, can be very illuminating.

Studies of the dialects spoken in the Netherlands show, as we might suspect, a complicated overlapping of many such cultural waves through the centuries. Although the dialect picture cannot always be induced to yield pinpoint accuracy, it does tend in a striking way to corroborate what we already know of cultural history: there has been for many centuries a strong prestige effect exerted by the western area that has left few features of the dialects of its neighbors unaffected. In at least two cases it has been claimed that this process of expanding influence reached such proportions that an earlier word or pronunciation survives only at the far edges of where the western influence extended. Two rather well-known examples have emerged from the work of the dialectologist G.G.Kloeke.[1] One shows that the second-person singular pronoun corresponding to *thou* in English and *du* in German survives today only in one or two pockets in the extreme Northeast of the Netherlands and on into Germany; Kloeke suggested that since all the other dialects use some form equivalent to the modern standard *jij* we have a picture here of western influence moving eastward. The other example appears to be even more striking. If we take a few very common words such as *ijs* and *tijd* 'ice, time' and *huis* and *muis* 'house, mouse' as representatives of many hundreds of other words pronounced today in the western region with diphthongs, and proceed to find out what the pronunciation is in dialects all over the Netherlands and Belgium, we discover an interesting pattern. Pronunciations of these same words with sounds like, respectively, the vowel in English *me* and in French *tu*, which we know for other reasons to have been the older pronunciations, are heard today in the eastern Netherlands provinces and in the western end of Flanders. This was interpreted by Kloeke, who went and listened to all these dialects personally, as a picture showing a great wave propagated by a prestige area in the middle, which could well have been Holland. Even more: this 'older' monophthong sound like French *tu* was itself a prestige wave that several centuries previously had begun somewhere in the western region and pushed back a still older sound like the vowel in English *too* until it is found today only at the extreme periphery of the Netherlands cultural area.[2]

The overall picture is much more complicated than all this suggests. Though we would of course like to agree with Kloeke that Amsterdam itself was the center from which this prestige expanded outward, this is anything but clear. We can certainly agree that in any case cultural history supports the dialect specialist's claim that the fashionable new pronunciations first arose in the southern cities of Antwerp and Brussels, both of which were flourishing cultural centers well before the latecomer Amsterdam. Though it may yet be proven that the dialect of Amsterdam itself lent certain of its features to neighboring ones in an ever widening circle, we would probably do better to look for a linguistic counterpart of the city's undeniable cultural magnetism in a slightly different realm. It was not so much down at the dialectal level that the rest of the country now began imitating the West but up at the level on which a new cultural game was beginning to be played, and the linguistic reflection of this was the formation of a common standard cultural language out of elements drawn from both North and South. It is in other words of crucial importance to know something about the language game being evolved in Amsterdam society at this period in cultural history.[3]

Fortunately the same cultural flourishing that brought commercial expansion and interest in science also brought a strong surge of interest, throughout Europe, in the languages spoken by the newly powerful 'third estate'. As early as 1550 an attempt was made in the Netherlands to establish a consistent orthography for a form of speech that was no longer the dialect of a single vest-pocket duchy but beginning to follow political reality by shaping itself into a compromise language intelligible over a wide area − again, something that was happening in all European countries in this time. This was followed by numerous orthographies, grammars, dictionaries and lists of native words meant as replacements for the Latin or French words now felt as blemishes on the mother tongue. One of the first to write in Dutch, as we can now begin to call the language, was Simon Stevin, who wrote an enthusiastic defense of the language and claimed it to be the most excellent for scientific writing. Stevin created many puristic words still in the language, for instance *hoofdstuk* 'chapter' and *beginsel* 'principle'. Stevin's tone is entirely characteristic: these works were not written with the detachment of natural scientists, but grammarians and lexicographers were deeply involved in the object of their investigations. One matter to which they give attention is just what we hoped to hear from them: there are so many new, fashionable pronunciations being used, they say, that it is difficult to know what to recommend; in particular there are noticeable differences in the way some people pronounce words like . . . *ijs* and *tijd, huis* and *muis*. A particularly intriguing study of the different ways in which the language was sorting out its various prestige items and crystallizing out a standard cultural language in this crucial period is Hellinga's *De opbouw van de algemeen beschaafde uitspraak van het Nederlands.*[4] In noticing how for the people writing in this time communication is not treated like a natural phenomenon but a cultural one subject to judgements of right and wrong, we have finally returned to our quest for the 'rules of the game': Let us take a closer look at one of the most brilliant of these treatises, the *Bericht van een niewe konst, genaemt de spreeckonst*, written by Petrus Montanus of Delft and published in 1635[5].

By the term *spreeckonst* Petrus Montanus means, roughly speaking, what we would call phonetics, and here he shows himself an observer of the order of a Huygens or Leeuwenhoek who has listened patiently to the speech of the urban centers but also poked around with his fingers to discover just what the speech organs were doing as he produced sounds. It was not at all obvious in his day that phonetics should be a separate branch of investigation, and so he takes the trouble to show its distinctness: language can be divided according to whether we are talking about hearing or seeing, that is speech or writing, and crossing this division there is the one that distinguishes qualities, that is from itself, from relations, that is signaling function.

Where speech and pure form intersect we have the *nieuwe konst*, the new art, called *spreeckonst*. The main part of the work, introduced by some charming dedicatory poems and a coy reference to the fact that he has hidden his name in its Dutch form in the title of his work (BERiCHt = Berg), is an exhaustive analysis of the sounds of the Dutch language as he knew it. Sounds are described in painstaking detail according to the organs involved in producing them and then according to the exact type of sounds they are, these are then shown to have different variations depending on the sorts of sequences in which the Dutch language happens to arrange them, and his description does not stop until he has gone on to describe the phonetic details of words, phrases and whole complex sentences. All this is developed by means of a highly idiosyncratic terminology that makes its interpretation today very difficult even for experts, but Montanus is able to point convincingly to the fact that he has arranged his terminology so as to reflect not the pronunciation of some fancied ideal language like Latin but that of the living language spoken every day by his society. Following the scientific fashion of his time, Montanus continually presents us with marvelously complicated and awesome-looking tables showing the relations of all the elements of a particular topic to each other. The most interesting aspect of Montanus' work to us, however, is not his observational skill, outstanding as this is, but the few pages he devotes to a discussion of how the act of communication takes place. In the interest of greater intelligibility to a modern reader, we will rearrange his presentation a bit.

The speech act, he says, is a complex one that is the result of a set of 'causes', some of them more observable than others. First of all (following his bent for tidy binary dichotomies) there are external and internal causes. Starting with the end result of language and working back, we have first of all the 'final cause', which is the message, what is expressed, that is the signifying function of language. Next is the 'efficient cause', which is the production of speech with a purpose, or the speaker himself who speaks as ultimately God directs. Coming to the internal causes, we have the 'formal cause' or the meaning that is imposed on spoken sound, and lastly the 'material cause' or the air or breath of speech. For his 17th-century contemporaries still at war with Spain, Petrus Montanus likens the relation between the internal and the external causes to the firing of a cannon and the result: the powder charge that impels the projectile is the breath that impels meaning, and the resulting trajectory of the cannonball is the message carried by speech on a set, purposeful course. These are quite plainly Aristotle's four causes, which had been ingeniously adapted to language by the Humanist Scaliger and were now being taken over by vernacular grammarians such as Petrus Montanus as a theoretical approach to their subject. In pure scientific terms this system is of course a failure; the real Renaissance *how* seems to lie in Petrus Montanus' articulatory observations which have little need of a blatantly unobjective attempt to explain the *why*. But this would ignore the vital fact that the language being scrutinized is a natural phenomenon only up to a point, and from there on it is a cultural artifact which has to be looked upon in some way that is meaningful to the culture. And Scaliger's 'cause' idea (intended only to apply to Latin) was singularly appropriate for this end. As it is adapted by Petrus Montanus to the cultural realities of the Dutch language spoken in 17th-century Holland, it says that the native vernacular consists of a material, the way 'we' pronounce it, that has a form impressed upon it that expresses the particular things 'we' want to say. In order for us to maintain our social identity as members of our culture, this language must be pronounced just right — hence the intense interest in phonetic description that comes just as the culture itself has reached a point of cohesion and independence. In terms of the cultural game, we can see that the culture itself, in its prestige speakers the ultimate arbiter of rightness, takes on a kind of 'sacred' aspect in the sense that its language must be conformed to and imitated with exact preciseness. The innermost rules of the game played by a culture are always felt to be natural and immutable. Accordingly, the language has to be recorded in grammars and dictionaries, much as sacred scripture itself is, and commented on and explained. In speaking, one is doing far more than merely communicating: in speaking in a certain accepted way — the way that Petrus Montanus tries to lay out in all its complexity — a person's very self-identity is involved, because he is participating in a very important game shared in by all members of the culture. In a very intensely direct way one presents oneself in his speaking, or as Erasmus said (though he shortsightedly thought only of Latin) one lives and develops in the qualities of his style.

A good bit of this last commentary is of course not to be found explicitly in Petrus Montanus, but it is plainly implied in his elaboration of the 'cause' theory as well as everywhere he insists on the rules the Dutch language follows. His work, and the many less idiosyncratic ones like it, leaves no room for doubt that the language spoken by the cultural elite of the 17th century was a vital cause of its group identity and every bit as important a monument to this successful interaction as were its political organization, its commercial enterprise, or the more visible cultural achievements we will see in the next chapter. The fixedness and standardization of the language now beginning to form a blanket over the dialects it had already shaped to its model represent the cultural game played by this class, and the rules of its speaking are the rules of social behavior that begin to be imitated throughout the domain of its influence.

The speech that formed the basis of this language was in the main that of Amsterdam, but with a strong enough admixture of fashionable pronunciations and words from the South that we find numerous writers of the time complaining about the scandalous spectacle of solid, straightforward Hollanders adopting the elegant manners and speech of the Brabanders in their midst. Few who lived at the time were able to view this rapid change with detachment. A social picture of unparalleled vividness is presented to us by the Amsterdam playwright and poet Bredero in *De Spaansche Brabander*, written in 1617. An affected 'nobleman' comes to Amsterdam speaking a strongly southern-flavored language and finds the Northerners with their boorish dialect a ridiculous spectacle indeed. Strictly as a dramatic work, Bredero's play is hardly more than moderately successful; it has rather the character of a series of lively, colorful canvases painted with an unexcelled ear for the pictorial resources of dialect and style. Bredero, a painter by profession, is not the first member of this culture to show a marked talent for creating paintings with words and portraits by allowing persons to come to life in their styles, and we will see that he is by no means the last.

The language of the 17th century was in the process of developing additional social dimensions. Whereas speech is remarkably conservative, retaining its manner of articulation and changing only slowly – the diphthongization that so radically altered its aspects and turned into a shibboleth of standardness was part of a slow development that took place independently in German and English as well – writing is far easier to bend to the demands of fashion, especially when it begins to take on a cultural independence of its own. In the Middle Ages writing was little more than a means of setting down speech, but after printing became well established and people became thoroughly accustomed to seeing things written down, writing became an important item in the cultural game: you can put on a written style just as you can put on elegant dress, a possibility that could not fail to appeal to the culture of the 17th century. In Holland of the 17th century, the raw material for the creation of the rules of this game came in the influx of an elegant form of language from the South, and this was borrowed and integrated into the style cultivated by people – largely members of the leisured Regent class – who wrote long letters to each other and created poems, essays and dramas until the result was an 'obligatory' written form of the language that was to be used as a badge of belonging to polite culture and that was quite distinct from everyday spoken language. Here we see the origins of an important cultural game, *spreektaal* versus *schrijftaal,* that members of Netherlands culture play to this day. The act of participation, in both its spoken form of conforming to a standard language – significantly called today *algemeen beschaafd* – and its written form of conforming to a distinct style, is one that was brought to maturity by 17th-century culture and that like many more superficial social habits has become permanently woven into the Dutch 'game'.

9 *A mythology of the visual*

Pieter Cornelisz. Hooft, a member of the Regent class whose father was a mayor of Amsterdam, was given the broad education expected by his peers, spent three years in Italy where his poetic ear picked up the new lyric style of the Renaissance, and at the age of 28 was given a largely honorific post at Muiden near Amsterdam which had the unsurpassed advantage of giving him the right to establish his residence in the historic Medieval castle there, the *Muiderslot*. The luster Hooft gave the castle over the next generation was to far surpass any it had acquired from the old days of knights and sieges. Here he held a literary court where poets, dramatists, artists, and statesmen such as Constantijn Huygens came together to discuss great ideas and inspire each other in their expression. The overriding concern that united all these people was how to develop an effective and at the same time esthetically pleasing means of expressing themselves in letters, poetry, dramas and exposition. They lived in an intensely visual age and in a visually very wide-awake culture, and they polished their control of the language until they could use words — many they would seldom use in everyday conversation — with maximum suggestive effect and, most important of all, with a sustained style that extended over whole pages and chapters. They developed their technique by writing long letters to each other — even when they lived close enough together that they could have talked in person — and together, under Hooft's leadership, they were the creators of a rich literary renaissance in the Netherlands. But the determined development of this new, visual kind

105

of language was not just another exercise in 17th-century vanity, as it is occasionally made out to be. The new visual style was meant (although the members of the *Muiderkring* might not have put it quite this way) as the only fitting way of expressing a number of lofty ideas that were in the air and that had to do with the very existence of the new Republic. In this union of high style and high ideal Hooft himself yielded to none. His *Nederlandsche Historiën*, one of the first examples of modern-sounding Dutch written prose, outlines in its long, elegant sentences the background and causes of the revolt of the Netherlands against the Spanish and the peculiar form of cooperation that resulted in the formation of the new state. While the Regents themselves were finding practical solutions to daily political problems, liberal thinkers like Hooft and, on a more abstract level, Hugo de Groot were responding to the challenge of finding a way of talking about the great new visions inherent in the democratic cooperation of equals.

Hooft's genius found an entirely different way of giving these ideas visual expression: putting them on the stage where they could be participated in not by reading but by seeing. The stage was a natural form of expression for the Regent class, whose culture was based to a great extent on the tastes of the old Chambers of Rhetoric, *Rederij-kerskamers,* that had a long tradition in the South going back into the Middle Ages; the prestige enjoyed by these proud cultivators of the mother tongue partly accounts for the ease with which their ornamented linguistic style migrated northward.[1] Hooft does not entirely escape from this: his plays have a spareness that contrasts strongly to the later Baroque tastes of even the Dutch stage, but they are populated by allegorical figures, choruses and lengthy declamatory speeches. In 1613, in the middle of the Truce period when religious strife was confronting the society with a crisis of alarming proportions, Hooft wrote *Geraerdt van Velsen.* Since it was hazardous to arouse the wrath of either party – as the fate of Oldenbarnevelt and De Groot was soon to prove – Hooft chose as a setting the Medieval history of his own *Muiderslot.* Floris V, Count of Holland, has violated the wife of Geraerdt van Velsen and ordered the execution of his brother, thereby breaking a cardinal rule that the sovereignty of the feudal lords under him must be respected. Geraerdt succeeds in capturing Floris, and together with his father-in-law and Gijsbert van Aemstel brings him to the Muiderslot. Meanwhile the figures Contention, Violence and Deception rise and urge the destruction of the country. After considerable heated discussion Gijsbert manages to talk Geraerdt out of delivering Floris into the hands of his enemies the English; during the night the ghost of the murdered brother comes to Floris and reproaches him, whereupon Floris, conscience-stricken, asks forgiveness of Geraerdt — which he is reluctant to grant. At dawn some of Floris' people come and release him, but they are attacked by a group of Geraerdt's people, and in the ensuing struggle Floris is killed by Geraerdt. The play concludes — to be sure, a bit anticlimactically to modern taste — with a long discourse by the figure of the river Vecht on the future glory of Amsterdam that is being prepared through all these difficulties.

This is plainly a political drama written for 1613. Both prince and the lords of the individual member states have their appointed areas, and there is prosperity in the state only as long as they work together harmoniously; when one betrays the confidence, the consequences are disastrous. Floris is of course guilty of intruding on the rights of Geraerdt and his brother, but Geraerdt is guilty too: he neglects his duty to his country for personal vengeance and seeks justice outside the established internal system. Even worse is the fact that the people intervene, with the result that a tragedy is precipitated. In the early years of the 17th century many were arguing that in the absence of a monarch sovereignty rested directly in the hands of the people, but Hooft sees only disorder there: order can not be created by a formless aggregation of individuals but only by people organized into states with duly constituted heads, who interact with enlightenment under a benign sovereign.[2] Hooft creates this person in Gijsbert, the wise statesman who tries to restore order without bloodshed, and the Stoic ideal of restraint in the cautious Machtelt, Geraerdt's wife. All these ideals put together give Hooft's picture of the political structure of the Dutch Republic as it should and could be.

It is customary to praise Hooft for the quality of his stage effects and the sharpness of his characters. Here he does indeed reach a height that is far above many of his contemporaries, and yet it is impossible to escape a feeling of impersonal woodenness in his characters, however strikingly they express themselves in flowing verse lines. Their representation of ideas emerges with force and clarity, but at the expense of our being able to experience them as full, many-sided individuals who refuse to be put into unidimensional molds. Undoubtedly Hooft's contemporary audiences did not expect this but were able to experience the characters as subordinated to the unity of the play's idea. In this the viewers were certainly aided to a great extent by the purely visual qualities of the central action on the stage.

The only literary member of the *Muiderkring* regularly heard of outside of the Netherlands is Joost van den Vondel, whose common rather than Regent origins made him a slightly discordant note in the circle's harmony. Though his colorful, Baroque tastes — usually ascribed to the Antwerp origins of his family — look oddly un-Dutch beside the cool, balanced Hooft, he probably deserves his greater place in history because he was just enough of an outsider to enter into the life of 17th-century Amsterdam with an enthusiasm that found expression in many volumes of poems and plays. It is interesting to compare Hooft's treatment of the conflict between Floris and Gijsbert or Gijsbrecht with a play written just a quarter of a century later, on the occasion of the dedication of the new theater in Amsterdam, but by sómeone who makes a similar point by way of a distinctly different set of symbols.

Gijsbrecht van Aemstel is defending Amsterdam against the besieger, Count Floris V — the action is based loosely on the historical fall of Amsterdam in 1304. In an encounter he captures a certain Vosmeer, who renounces his allegiance to Floris and asks for acceptance by

Gijsbrecht. He is joyfully received and given the important task of guarding a ship tied just outside the city walls. But the ship's hold contains enemy soldiers, and Vosmeer is really a spy planted by Floris to gain access to the city. In the evening, when everyone is at church because it is Christmas night, Vosmeer brings the ship into the city and the troops emerge and begin taking it, opening the gates to Floris' main force which had only pretended to retreat. Gijsbrecht engages them but is forced back until he is faced with a surrender ultimatum. Though concerned about the fate of his family he places the good of his people above his own personal survival and is dissuaded from rejecting the ultimatum only by the appearance of the archangel Raphael, who commands him to flee eastward to Prussia and there found a city named Holland, comforting him with a promise of the future greatness of Amsterdam.

Here we have the puzzling spectacle of a main character who is halfway between a historical personage and a mythological eponymous hero, who bravely does his best but who without any clear act of tragic guilt ends in humiliating failure. What kind of a myth could Vondel be telling in this drama? The key is to be found exactly where it was in Hooft's drama: the individual as such counts for nothing, and the society itself is everything. In Vondel the raw material of the story passed through the creative intellect of a long-time Arminian who more and more found symbolic meaning in the mythological past and who was eventually to convert to Catholicism. God's plan is concerned with institutions and not with individuals and this plan had foreordained the splendor of Amsterdam in the 17th century; no mere individual can interfere with this no matter how noble his intentions are. Gijsbrecht is not a rebellious Faust but a symbol of Dutch culture itself in his realization that the individual's true fulfillment is not as an ethical island but as an integrated member of a larger whole.

Like Hooft, Vondel used an event that was part of the heritage of the Netherlands to communicate to his society an important truth about its culture in a form that was thoroughly meaningful to it: the double means of elegant verbal style and appealing stage effects. In an even more undisguised way than Hooft, Vondel created a myth when he made his characters little more than thin cardboard figures standing for the symbolic ideas of the play. There is good reason for calling him an epic poet rather than a dramatist. He seems to have been incapable of seeing the human personality in any other way than with a touching, almost childlike simplicity and directness of significance, qualities which made him a born mythmaker to his culture – a status eloquently attested to by the fact that *Gijsbrecht van Aemstel* has enjoyed a revival in recent times and in its traditional annual production in Amsterdam has shown the cyclic character of true myth. But for all their grandeur and their success in capturing a genuinely Dutch myth, Hooft and Vondel were failures in the larger sense that they fell short of the universality of all truly meaningful myths, and this is assuredly not because their work resists translation. It is because they tried to communicate the myth of the ethical and social setting, a large-scale idea that clashed fatally with the inescapable demands of the overwhelmingly individualistic stage. The impulse of the viewer to identify with the persons he sees in front of him had to be constantly thwarted in order to remind him of a larger, more abstract ideal not shown on the stage, and this unresolved tension between subject matter and medium denied their attempts the unity that is prerequisite to all great art.

A cultural ideal that focuses on the importance of belonging in a large framework, whether this be concrete and observable or abstract and understood, needs for its expression not the transitory immediacy of the spoken word but the detached permanence of artifacts that can depict on a large scale and yet be grasped all at once. The culture supported painters in very large numbers, and paintings were demanded not by the Church or wealthy princes but by ordinary, individual citizens. The popularity of paintings far exceeded that of the theater and probably extended to a greater proportion of the population. This popularity was due, we are usually told, to the fact that these confident, well-to-do people loved seeing around them faithful reflections of themselves and their surroundings; much as if our culture were to demand that high-quality photographs of all aspects of it be on constant display in houses and public places. The very ubiquity of paintings in the 17th century suggests that this is rather too shallow an interpretation, unless we are willing to believe that we are dealing with an unprecedentedly narcissistic culture. Paintings must certainly have meant to those who created them, however mediocre some of them were, and to those who paid for them, however little artistic discrimination many of them may have had, something of a deeper symbolic significance. They were treated by the culture not like practical objects such as stoves but more like the myths a culture insists on having repeated over and over because they have concealed in them at some deeper level a message the whole culture participates in. This surface appeal that contains a profound cultural function beneath it is the subject of an intriguing remark made by Timmers in *Kleine atlas van de Nederlandse beschaving*[3] :

In één stil genrestuk van Vermeer zit meer poëzie dan in al de grote decors van het Raadhuis, één vergezicht van Van Goyen, Ruysdael of Philips Koninck maakt alle Hollandse mythologieën overbodig.*

Superfluous, for the simple reason that these paintings are themselves the mythology of an intensely visual culture. Our final task before we leave the 17th century will be to consider how medium and myth are united here into a permanent contribution to Western civilization.

All of these artists ultimately attended the school of the Flemish Primitives, the painters who in an uncanny way were able to translate form, texture, depth and color onto a flat surface. The Medieval Flemish painters rendered everything with a minute, devoted attention that made it a heroic struggle to subordinate this seething

---

* There is more poetry in one quiet genre painting of Vermeer than in all the grandiose decor of the [Amsterdam] City Hall: one panorama of Van Goyen, Ruysdael or Philips Koninck makes all Dutch mythologies superfluous.

multitude of things into a single visual image, but by the 17th century their descendents have learned how to do this. Everything the painter sees is still faithfully rendered with consummate care, but the difference is that now everything in the canvases — some of them by now of awesome proportions — relates directly and logically to everything else; no longer do all the symbolically important things in the painting crowd and jostle each other. The painter no longer attempts to illuminate everything with more or less equal intensity but has learned how to use light in so natural a way that instead of inviting the viewer to participate symbolically in his painting he brings him in physically by making him feel that he is actually present in it. But rather than indulge any further in generalities about 17th century art which can be found in even the most modest art history text, let us derive our lesson from a brief look at just three paintings out of the nearly endless array we have to choose from. Since our only purpose will be to take a slightly different look at things that are already familiar, we will risk the danger of falling into cliché and choose works for which reproductions are readily available, by painters whose individual style is easily recognizable: Frans Hals, Johannes Vermeer and Jacob van Ruysdael.[4]

Hals immediately brings to mind the *schutterstuk,* the showy group portrait of military officers that the Dutch invented and that Hals raised to a peak of artistic expression. But let us avoid these for the same reason we will later avoid the seascape: their Dutchness is so obvious that it might get in the way of our penetrating a little ways below their surfaces, and in any case a meaningful discussion of the complicated arrangement and symbolism of a *schutterstuk* would take us quite beyond our modest aim here. An achievement of at least equal dimensions but one that makes a very somber impression is Hals' group portrait of the Governesses of the Home for the Aged. Standing in front of these five old ladies requires a respectful silence: before you there sit five very strong and individual personalities, each face more forbidding than the next, all dressed soberly and looking out from their dark interior without any flashes of really bright color.

But you are unable to experience any one exclusive of the rest; her figure always draws the other four to your eye. The same light that comes from the left is illuminating all of them in the same way, highlighting their faces, collars, cuffs and hands and letting the rest recede into the background. These highlights are arranged with such skill that they form a chain holding the five figures together, and the group is closed off on the left by the slightly raised hand and on the right by the standing figure looking toward the center. Discovering more and more of these unifying touches can be a fascinating game. If you follow the natural impulse one feels on looking at a Van Eyck painting and move close to the canvas to see just how fine the detail is, Hals always forces you to step back again. The textures that at a distance seemed realistic turn into broad, hasty-looking meaningless dabs of the brush, so you inevitably retreat to the point closer than which the painter knows you are unable to participate in the scene as a whole. Hals seems to be telling a myth here in two ways: first, a keen, penetrating observation is important, and the visual aspects of what you see hold profound meaning. In the case of these five persons, the meaning in the character dicovered in each one by Hals' unsparing eye and rendered for the viewer to read just as he can do in the people around him. Hals can even be said to be, like all of the best Dutch painters, the artistic voice of the contemporary scientists who proceeded on the assumption that it is through the eye that truth must come and all other avenues must be ultimately submitted to its test. Second, things are meaningful in their appropriate setting. The five figures belong in an artistically unified whole, but the contemporary viewer would have known this only subconsciously. What he knew consciously was that he was present in front of a group of members of his society such as he could see daily, surrounded with all the attributes of their rightful function – not symbolic objects surrounding them as in a Van Eyck painting, but as they were ordinarily experienced in manner of dress and posture. There is a distinct satisfaction in meeting five formidable ladies who are at the job of helping to keep one's society going and therefore contributing to one's own life in however indirect a way.

There is undoubtedly a certain amount of tension between the dominating Dutch myth of the centrality of the social setting and the
constant Renaissance tendencies of the personalities seen by the
penetrating eye of a Hals to burst out of this setting. This tension is
kept in balance by Hals and provides the vitality not found in the
work of lesser artists, but in the case of Rembrandt the intense inner
meaning of each person, thing and arrangement so completely bursts
out of the frame of this myth that Rembrandt's universal message
must be considered as if it were something that almost completely
transcends the culture that produced it. Moving back in the other
direction, we find that most of the 17th-century painters were content to represent interiors with people in them who so little stand
out from them that their names have long since been forgotten. The
great prophet of the interior scene was of course Vermeer, whose
painting The Milkmaid will be our example, though just about any
other of his paintings would do as well.

We are witnesses to the most unspectacular scene imaginable. In the
corner of a somewhat barren-looking room a robust, plainly dressed
girl is pouring some milk out of a pitcher into a pot. A number of
trivial objects lying around and hanging on the wall such as baskets
and jars give additional evidence that she is a maid doing kitchen
work. So photographically real is the light that comes through the
window at the upper left and plays on the maid, the trickle of milk
and the broken pieces of bread that we ought to be able to feel, smell
and taste what we see. And yet nobody ever really saw a scene like
this. Though the maid has a plain face that shows no particular
personality and in any case is turned downward so that we are unable
to see the eyes, she dominates the scene absolutely. She stands a little
to the right of the center, bound in a completely natural way to the
left side of the picture by the obvious – almost harsh – light source,
but yet not cutting the picture off at the right even though the
straight line of her back very nearly does this. She is turned a little
toward the right, and her head is turned just a trifle more in this
direction, a little beyond where it would need to be to look straight at

the pitcher; this is a hint that points in the direction of the charcoal foot-warmer on the floor that humbly closes off the composition. The line formed by her implied look and her arms leads directly past its climax at the white milk against the dark background, and on to the cluster of objects on the table. The wooden foot-warmer is balanced at the upper left by the basket on the wall and the polished can just below it, so that the entire arrangement forms, in a completely unassuming way, a large X. Exactly the same sort of sophisticated balance can be found in the colors, which are subdued and delicate but give us a curiously cool, detached sensation and carry a significant message when all taken together. Vermeer too tells a myth about observation, though in a dialect that is different than that of Hals. Through the subtle transformations that have taken place in the artist's consciousness, all the elements in a thoroughly familiar scene have been united in a single impression that conveys the message that the most everyday setting is yet of transcendent importance – precisely because it is an everyday setting. Vermeer's observational skill and feeling for arrangement have raised the familiar to the status of a symbol that can be participated in directly and immediately. The maid's action and the attributes of her occupation all take on the same symbolic import that the crowded objects of the Medieval religious painters did, with the difference that here the underlying myth is not the Christian mystery but the cultural ideal of a mysterious, hidden quality permeating and sustaining everyday life. There is nothing left of the Medieval concept that each act and each thing had a direct line to the eternal, but instead the maid with her objects reminds the participant in the painting that the culture she too belongs to only makes sense because it consists of people in a meaningful interaction with each other and with the surroundings. Whatever is taken out of its setting loses its significance, its magic light.

Even the apparently unlimited talent of the 17th-century painters could not render an entire social setting, but it could and did enable the viewer to participate in a very closely related type of setting, the natural surroundings of the country itself. There is possibly· no finer example of their startling ability to put the very feel of the air onto canvas than Ruysdael's painting of Haarlem as seen from the dunes at Overveen. This painting might better be called a skyscape than a landscape, because well over two thirds of the entire canvas is devoted to the sky, the scene· itself lying down at the bottom of the painting. Here we are standing on the dunes that edge the western coast, and the modest rise of perhaps fifty feet enables us to look off to the east into a distance that never seems to end. The entire sky is filled with dark, brooding clouds of the type that move along rapidly, changing their shape in the wind. Most of the ground is under the somber shadow of these thick clouds, but here and there a fitful spot of wan sunlight has broken through. There is one on the dunes at our feet, another large one on some of the houses in the foreground, another at the right in the middle distance, and some of the buildings of Haarlem on the horizon are also highlighted in the pale light. The sunlit houses at the left foreground stand out starkly against the dark trees and the unillumined house directly behind, and balancing this on the right, a little farther back, a house in darkness is silhouetted against the bright fields behind in which the arms of some windmills catch the sun. This painting offers a remarkable experience in its tangibility: we stand looking off into the immeasurable distance even beyond Haarlem, where on the distant horizon steeples and trees stand out sharply. The air is clear, and yet we can feel its heavy, chilly wetness that puts shades of gray in all the colors of the trees, grass and houses and blends them all into a single impression. This tangible feeling of an overwhelming spaciousness which is filled dramatically with things that its damp weight binds together is accented by our knowledge of the presence of the wind: we feel that the sunny spots are flickering and hurrying along the ground, and we can see a group of birds high in the sky dashing along in front of the clouds. Only a native of the Lowlands would know that the artist has here not created something dramatic but simply depicted a perfectly ordinary day in Holland with its low landscape and correspondingly high skies always chilly and full of the threat of rain. People play hardly any role at all in this painting.

116

A few are discernable in the foreground performing farm tasks, but elsewhere their presence is implied rather than real. The huge bulk of the St. Bavo church in the center of Haarlem rises all the more awesomely because of the heavy mistiness of the air. The viewer participates in this painting by knowing where he is and being able to sense again the peculiar qualities of the natural surroundings, the setting, with all its brooding monumentality heightened and filled with portent by the artist's unifying eye, in which life takes place. A great many Dutch painters succeeded, in paintings like this one, in creating a majestic spaciousness and so in telling the myth that all things have their appointed and indispensable setting, but only a very few geniuses of the stature of Ruysdael were able to suffuse the entire setting with a magical atmosphere that turned the ultimate setting, the world itself as they experienced it, into a symbolic expression of their culture's deeply held conviction that life 'as we live it' has a luminous quality for those able to grasp it. These few are the true mythmakers of their culture, and it is their completely harmonious blending of this abstract ideal with the pictorial medium so appreciated by their visual culture that justifies the place they occupy in the history of Western Civilization.

A word or two of epilogue might be forgivable at this point. The pictorial style of cultural expression extended far beyond its true domain in painting and thoroughly permeated Dutch verbal expression throughout its history, particularly in the realm of lyric poetry, a genre with a distinguished tradition that we are ignoring here in its entirety. Almost three centuries after Ruysdael, the exact same feeling of the landscape was captured again by the poet Marsman in a few sentimental lines known to every Dutch citizen:

117

Denkend aan Holland
zie ik brede rivieren
traag door oneindig
laagland gaan,
rijen ondenkbaar
ijle populieren
als hoge pluimen
aan den einder staan;

en in de geweldige
ruimte verzonken
de boerderijen
verspreid door het land,
boomgroepen, dorpen,
geknotte torens,
kerken en olmen
in een groots verband . . .*

Many artists and poets painted the *geweldige ruimte,* and a few with true vision captured the untranslatable *groots verband* that is its underlying meaning. Without a grasp of the significance of the *verband,* whether this is meant to imply the natural environment, religion, a political ideal or even a society supported by *zuilen,* the culture of the Netherlands as it crystallized out in the 17th century can not be properly understood.[5]

* Thinking of Holland, I see broad rivers leisurely moving through endless lowland, rows of unimaginably wispy poplars standing like tall plumes on the horizon; and immersed in the enormous space, the farms spread through the land, clusters of trees, villages, squat towers, churches and elms, in a single grand setting.

10 Literary reflections

All three of the paintings we just finished considering were executed after 1650, the date that is usually felt to mark the approximate beginning of the slow decline of the Republic's vitality. Our pursuit of cultural expression has carried us right on past a historical period of uninterrupted turbulence. After the Truce there were several further engagements with the Spanish, a challenge which did not prevent an increasingly widening split between the two factions on whose uneasy sharing of power the viability of the Republic rested, on the one hand the States General, the instrument of the Regents, and on the other the stadhouders. The influence and popularity of the latter increased under Maurits and, after his death in 1625, Frederik Hendrik. But when Frederik Hendrik died in 1647, the year before the conclusion of peace, the opposition between the two forces had sharpened to such an extent that his short-lived successor William II left control in the hands of the Regents, who embarked on two decades of rule without a stadhouder. This was a period of growing rivalry with the English which broke out in armed conflict in 1652 and again in 1665.

But such a neglect of the historical chain of events is not without some justification in a discussion that focuses on cultural history. In all the centuries prior to around the first quarter of the 17th, political events are very much in the foreground for the simple reason that they are the circumstances to which the people of the Netherlands respond with a group of independent provinces and eventually with a republic embodying a unique way of life for its citizens. At the same

119

time, a number of obscure social predispositions in this population gives shape to the foreground history in insisting on 'privileges' and later fumbling its way toward a tolerance that makes possible for the first time on the European stage the appearence of an entire state based on the 'free association of equals. It would be presumptuous to try to give either one of these two opposite influences causal precedence over the other. But once the response has taken what seems to be permanent form, we begin to feel that the dynamic relation between historical event and cultural creativity has ended and that the events themselves are now background, exercising little formative influence on a response that has proved its viability. Unfortunately, the other side of this particular coin is that a culture no longer in a dynamic state of formation ceases to do much more shaping of the historical events in their larger pattern.

The very success of this grand *pays sans frontières* – to recall Wilson's phrase – that made it the home of a great debate on Cartesianism and prepared the ground for many further contributions to philosophy and science also opened it in its more static phase to a flood of outside cultural influence. So great does the receptivity of the culture of the Netherlands become, especially to cultural pressure from France, that by the third quarter of the 17th century histories of Dutch culture unfailingly adopt either a lamely apologetic tone or an archly patronizing one that makes it difficult for a student of the culture to maintain his interest at a high pitch. Let it be freely admitted that after sometime around the 1670's the cultural originality of the Netherlands faded so rapidly that with a few outstanding exceptions such as Hobbema in the field of painting we are hard pressed to find much that was not done at least as well elsewhere, and often better. The field of interest we have staked out for ourselves frees us from any obligation to concentrate on cultural manifestations of universal proportions – quite the contrary, we noted a chapter or two ago that in fact it obliges us to cautiously avoid this universality unless we are fortunate enough to be able to point out an unambiguous cultural message in it. We are still engaged in the modest enterprise of tracing the rules of the cultural game, and we can be confident they continue through the next three centuries if only because so much of the present reminds us of the 17th century. The question is thus merely where we should now look for reflections of the rules.

In Chapter 8 we put to work the fact that there is probably no cultural manifestation that so faithfully follows the lines and bounds of the culture itself as the language. We found there and in the first part of the next chapter that the literature written in this language — at least certain of the most widely acclaimed works — had a grandiose flourish to it that matched the confidence of the times but was nevertheless so preoccupied with reflecting cultural rules as to rob itself of extracultural significance. The literary histories assure us — sometimes only between the lines — that in spite of the fact that literary expression in the two centuries following the Golden Age was inundated by outside influence, particularly French and English, the literature produced in the Dutch language reflects a consistently provincial outlook that remains determinedly Dutch through all the changing fashions. This gives evidence of being just what we need in order to view the culture of the Netherlands through the eyes of its members. It might even turn out that precisely this social faithfulness is the particular genius of the literature of the Netherlands, and that some of it looks undistinguished in European eyes partly because the wrong standards have been applied to it.

There is no escaping the fact that the rules we are looking for are, after all, changing only very slowly now. This, plus the fact that we must resist the temptation to allow the whole history of the literature to pass in review, suggests that we might most profitably follow the continued course of historical events and stop every now and then to take a sounding in the literature to see how it serves as a reflection of what the society is thinking. Rather than stop every ten or twenty years for a very superficial consideration of a literary work, we will gain more insight by spacing the stopping places out more and examining fewer works in greater detail. It happens, by pure chance, that a span of some sixty years will enable us to take giant steps through historical continuity and also take into consideration several of the works that Dutch culture itself has proclaimed to be its masterpieces. This approximate 60 year cycle will be a convenient device to us only as long as we do not regard it as possessed of any deeper significance whatever.[1]

If we begin at 1613, the year in which Hooft's *Geraerdt van Velsen* appeared, a step of 58 years takes us to 1671, by general agreement the outer limit of the true Golden Age and the year of publication of Jan Luyken's *Duytsche Lier*. Luyken's family was Remonstrant, though before his birth his parents abandoned this sect in favor of a stricter one that emphasized the principles of moral living. He was trained as an artist and excelled in the field of etching, producing in such abundance that thousands of his etchings are still preserved. In spite of the sobriety of his upbringing, however, Luyken was strongly attracted to the vain pastime of poetry and while still quite young managed to embarrass his family – and some pious literary historians since then – by publishing a volume of enthusiastic love poetry, the *Duytsche Lier*. Only a few years after this he appears to have thought the better of it, because for the rest of his life he confined himself to the writing of fervently religious poetry denouncing earthly vanity. For all its puritanism, though, the 17th century was not Victorian, and public taste in general found nothing incompatible in eroticism and sobriety merged into a single outlook. Coming in the late 17th century, a time when personal sentiment is usually heavily encrusted with stylistic ornamentation, the *Duytsche Lier* stands out from all the rest because of the freshness, originality and taste of its lyric expression. On the other hand it was almost (though not quite) inevitable that a professional engraver should have found poetry a natural form of expression, inasmuch as his culture insisted that all ideas had first to be grasped visually; this turned poetic expression into little more than elaborations on an explicit or understood picture of the idea.[2] The *Duytsche Lier* consists of ten groups of poems, each group introduced by an engraving showing allegorically one aspect of love and a couple of lines of verse explaining the theme, whereupon the poems that follow explore various elaborations of this theme. The first engraving, for instance, shows a woman representing Melancholy and a figure called Amor who has taken a torch from her hand and extinguished it in a nearby stream. The accompanying verse says

De liefde is stark genoeg om droefheit te overwinnen;
Haar smeulend vuur verdrenkt hij in de vloet der minne.*

The poems that follow this and the other nine symbolic emblems take up a whole range of emotions from the passionate to the austere, most of them directly or indirectly influenced by classical theories of the various roles of love. Though they specify tunes and are thus meant to be sung, an evidence of audial immediacy that modern taste has abandoned, they are pictorially vivid and never allow their dominant visuality to fade. Not only is Luyken speaking with the voice of his culture — or perhaps rather painting with its brush — in validating experience through the eye, he is also faithful to some of its deeper convictions. Even the most sweepingly erotic of the verses know exactly where the line is drawn: there is a boundary of taste set by the superior claims of morality that he never goes beyond. Indeed, in some of the poems in the later sections of the collection he jeopardizes his tone of freshness and charm by hinting strongly that thoughts of passion outside of the proper marriage ties are an evil mirage, leading some later commentators to wonder whether he was already beginning to recant here. But this seems like too crude an explanation. Jan Luyken gives vivid expression to the colorful sensuality of 17th-century European culture, but immediately below the surface he remains a sturdily moralistic Netherlander who feels the exact same obligation all his cultural ancestors felt to teach his contemporaries a useful lesson.

* Love is strong enough to conquer melancholy; / He quenches its smoldering fire in the stream of passion.

Unfortunately it is all too appropriate to call Luyken's robust confidence the very last reflection of the true Golden Age. The very next year, 1672, saw the assassination of the two foremost Regents and the beginning of the nearly disastrous third English war that brought a decisive end to the self-assured prosperity and security of the Republic. These hostilities involved such a formidable alliance of enemies, all pledged to the destruction of the Republic and the dividing up of the spoils, that the situation would have been entirely hopeless except for the fact that one of these enemies was Louis XIV of France; it was mainly a fear of French imperialism that mobilized enough support on the side of the Republic to enable it to survive. Although peace with England was concluded the next year, the unprepared Republic had managed to organize its military resources rapidly enough that the struggle with the French could be carried on for another five years. During the whole third quarter of this century the antagonism between the Regents and the stadhouders had reached a climax; the Regents had attempted to exclude the Orange family entirely, but popular unrest forced them to back down – a symbol of popular limitations on the power of the Regents was felt to be indispensible. This stadhouder was William III, who in the sharpened religious turbulence that accompanied Louis' revocation of the Edict of Nantes in 1685 – the formal promise of religious liberty in France – and the accession of James II in England in the same year found himself in the front line of defense against France and, in 1689, called to England to replace the Catholic James as king. The new war with the French did not come to an end until 1697.

The military imperialism of France did not prevent the accompanying cultural one that flooded the Netherlands as it did the rest of Europe, bringing with it in its early stages a strong interest not only in manners and styles but in the new ideas being developed there that had to do with the overriding importance of reason in the understanding of the world and the conduct of human life. This is too much a part of the general European heritage to need review here. Somewhat less familiar is the role played by England. In spite of some surface appearances, the cultural habits and values of England and the Netherlands ran in remarkably similar directions, and the repeated wars they fought have much more the aspect of lovers' quarrels than of the deeply bitter struggles between the Dutch and the Spanish. The sea skirmishes for commercial advantage did not prevent constant traffic between the countries from the monarchic level on down to the common. John Locke, the writer on tolerance and explorer of the mechanics of the human understanding, was only one of many who found a congenial home in the Netherlands in the 1680's and the succeeding decades.

By the early years of the 18th century a solidly entrenched and continually spreading bourgeois, middle-class spirit had come to dominate Dutch society even more thoroughly than it had in the culture's heyday, and this class found an ideal expression of its orderly, confident prejudices in the application of reason to all aspects of life. One ordinary Dutch citizen who went to England, observed polite life there and returned to bring some of its useful features to his own culture was Justus van Effen, who in 1731, just 59 years after Luyken's little masterpiece, began publishing his *Hollandsche Spectator.* This was an obvious and admitted imitation of Addison and Steele, but its noteworthiness comes in the shrewd ways in which Van Effen adapted the idea to the specific needs in his own culture. As we would expect, a great many of the essays he wrote during the span of four years are directly moralistic, such as his *Vertoog over beschaving* outlining the ways in which Reason is always able to distinguish what is good, or the large number that offer common-sense commentary on the contemporary social scene. He did this in a simple, unassuming prose that is a direct reflection of his readers' preference for a proper avoidance of self-assertion. Tastes have changed radically in this half-century; this cultivated, detached prose inevitably seems a bit flat next to the effervescent outpourings of a Jan Luyken, but its very sustained and deliberate coolness makes it a more suitable medium for reflecting the inner dimensions of a whole society than the irrepressible individualism of drama and lyric. And this is precisely what Van Effen found himself doing, becoming adept at setting down his

125

observations and so adopting the role of forerunner of a long tradition of socially oriented prose narrative. Van Effen carried his observing well beyond the realm of social commentary, into the description of individual character and social interaction. He developed this to such an extent that many of the resulting vignettes completely burst out of the bounds set by a semi-journalistic weekly essay series and take on an independent life as complete stories. Let us pause for a moment's look at two of the most famous of these.

The story called *Thijsbuurs os,* which can be rendered as something like 'Neighbor Matthew's ox', tells about Thijs, who works for a shoemaker and buys an ox which he then slaughters. This is all that happens. But the charm is in the way it is told: Thijs himself tells it in a rambling, colloquial style that shows his naive pleasure at the whole series of events and his almost outlandish pride in being the center of attention. He recounts with obvious delight how his boss and he go into the deal together, go to the field to choose a fat animal, drink a great deal of wine to seal their agreement and finally take the ox to Thijs' house when the shoemaker's wife objects to the fuss. Thijs insists on delivering the blow himself as the butchers admire the quality of the ox, and he wins a wager with his neighbors on how much the meat will weigh. There is no 'point' to the story other than the complete naturalness and appropriateness with which everything happens and the pleasure the reader derives from seeing the whole detailed scene through Thijs' and ultimately Van Effen's eyes. The observational invitation contained in the very word 'spectator' is such a natural extension of Dutch cultural values that one wonders why they did not think of this genre first.

Equally characteristic is a little idyll Van Effen called *Burgervrijage* but which commonly goes by the name *Kobus en Agnietje.* This one is openly moralistic, beginning with the author's introductory comment that declarations of love are high-order achievements of human life. The Spectator then tells how one day when he has sitting unobserved behind his window an acquaintance began across the street between

126

Agnietje, the hard-working but poor daughter of a widow, and Kobus, a successful young carpenter who is socially a bit above her level. She is of course flattered by his attention but too embarrassed to admit it. After that Agnietje refuses to appear when Kobus strolls by, and he resorts to bringing his sister to help him break the ice. This works so well that soon Kobus and Agnietje have serious intentions with respect to each other. The Spectator himself assures Kobus' worried father that Agnietje is fully worthy of his son's attention, and a meeting of both families is arranged. For a while it looks as though the deal is off when Agnietje's mother declares that the union would only be proper with a dowry that she is unable to provide, but this difficulty is resolved, everybody – including the ubiquitous Spectator – dissolves in tears, and the story concludes with an elaborate celebration.

Van Effen's Rationalistic point is quite obvious: every person is possessed of an innate dignity that has nothing to do with outward ornament or social station. The two main characters by their being on different social levels and nevertheless falling in love exemplify the respect that triumphs over intolerance. The idea that true civilization comes from within and that everyone is potentially equal in respect to it is, to be sure, not a specific invention of the culture of the Netherlands. But the ideal of reasonableness and toleration was one to which Dutch middle-class readers had long been accustomed, and the plain implication that people in rational interaction can find the right standards of behavior played once again the culture's fundamental tone. Van Effen was a popular writer, and was deservedly proud of his ability to depict familiar scenes with words. In 1733, a few months after the appearance of *Kobus en Agnietje,* he grudgingly acknowledges many letters of praise, but remarks concerning the reader,

't geen hem in die stukjes behaagt heeft, is blotelijk geweest de levendige getrouwheid van de schilderye*

* What pleased him in these pieces was merely the lively faithfulness of the painting.

and with the truculent word 'merely' indicates that such people have missed the main point, which in all these stories is the moral itself. The story of Thijs may be amusing to read, but the author's trouble has been in vain unless we understand it as a skillful way of clothing the useful moral about sticking to one's proper concerns. In his ever-present, keen-eyed role in the game of the Spectator, observing and painting but also assuming the role of the teacher of guidelines for the practical living of life, Van Effen creates another myth and innocently transforms himself into a modest-sized culture hero.

If we were to adopt a metaphor to account for the stages of development we find in the bourgeois life style that is a unique expression of the main generative forces in the culture of the Netherlands, we could with some justice pick the well-worn image of the course of the day. Some very clear preparatory stages in the Middle Ages notwithstanding, this development really dawns in the 1590's, proceeds through its early morning stages in the experimental and formative decades of the Golden Age, and by now has reached the late morning when its imprint is pervading more and more segments of the population. As long as we do not take this oversimplified metaphor too literally, it will prove to be a useful means of putting the social events of the next few chapters into a certain perspective.

11 Noontime:
Sara Burgerhart

The reflection of social realities that we find in painting and literature is not always an accurately balanced one. In the first half of the 18th century some evidence of discontent with society breaks through and finds expression, but the overwhelming impression we get is one of contented and almost soporific peace: things tend to have a polite, French look about them and everyone seems to be wearing the wigs that give this whole period its customary name *pruikentijd*. While this pretty accurately reflects a comfortable affluence enjoyed by the upper half of society, it masks some dramatic things that were going on under the surface.

A major share of the blame for the social malaise of this time has to be laid at the doorstep of a situation that has a long history in the Netherlands, the balance of power between the Regents as representatives of the interests of the privileged classes and the stadhouder as representative of the population at large. This relation had always been a source of considerable tension, but whereas in the time of Prince Maurits and Oldenbarnevelt the tension had been a fruitful one – however tragic its outcome –, it now seemed to be increasingly inclined to drain away the creative energy of the society. When William III died in 1702 in England, the Netherlands provinces were again left without a stadhouder, a situation the Regents tried in every way they could to perpetuate. The tightly-knit unity that had characterized the Republic during its most successful period decayed, the seven provinces more and more going their separate ways and

129

jealously preserving their independence from Holland. The chaos and disorder of this time would have been much worse if power had not been in the hands of a few talented and far-sighted officials in the Council of State. But widespread discontent over economic ills such as flagrant exploitation by corrupt tax officials and unemployment refused to disappear, because it was rooted in the realization that during nearly the whole first half of the century there was no real counterbalance to the authority of the Regents in a state whose very existence was predicated on a delicate balance of almost equally weighted interests. It was not until 1747, deep in the desperate situation brought on by the War of the Austrian Succession, a struggle with France that directly threatened the Republic's survival, that a wave of popular demand forced the Regents to name another stadhouder, who became William IV. Not only did the office now bring increased powers, but it became hereditary and national for the first time, moving the state a small step closer to the dynastic monarchy the Regents found such a nightmare. William's authority as an heir to the prestigious Orange title was more symbolic than real, even if this symbolic function was a crucially important one at the time.[1] His leadership was weak, and the sharp decline in his prestige took with it the former esteem for his whole family as a proper crusader against the hated Regents. It is easy to see that without some radical changes, a situation like this in which large segments of the population are left without any proper representation of their interests will provide a dangerous amount of fuel for revolution.

Around the middle of the century increasing numbers of prints, pamphlets and poems show the active presence of those who took up this challenge: the 'Patriots'. In the whole second half of the 18th century increasing numbers of people were debating the chief intellectual question of the time, the possibility of founding society on justice and reason. Questions such as the nature of man and language, the origin of society and its essential features preoccupied most of this century, and came to a climax toward its end in the writings of Voltaire, Rousseau and the French *encyclopédistes*. The Dutch

Patriots took up these ideas and provided a voice for the growing frustration in the country, gaining power until they exercised direct control in some cities, particularly in Holland, and changing the social alignment in the country from a 2-way split into a 3-way one. The Patriots now formed a powerful third force that was out of sympathy with the English-oriented stadhouder William IV and his son and successor William V, and of course implacably opposed to the Regents, the *ancien régime* which they felt, with considerable justice, to be outdated, rigid and undemocratic. Toward the end of the century events succeed each other with a fateful rush: in 1780 the Dutch again found themselves in a war with England, unpopular in spite of widespread sympathy with the American revolutionaries; the gap between stadhouder and people became so wide that in 1787 Prussian troops had to be called in to restore order, whereupon Patriots in considerable numbers fled the country feeling that oppression had settled in for good. In 1789 came the French Revolution, but the Netherlands found itself officially on the side of England and Austria against France. When the French declared war in 1792 and invaded the Netherlands, they were welcomed as liberators by a great many people who saw the possibility of a workable balance of interests only in an adherence to French revolutionary ideals and thus felt the 'invaders' to be more truly national in spirit than their own legally constituted government. In 1795 William V fled to England, largely unnoticed and unregretted, and the Republic of the seven provinces came to an end.

Many of the people who fled the Netherlands in 1787 did not find their lives or liberty in direct danger but were engaging in a forceful demonstration of disaffection with the way things were going at home. Two of these were Elizabeth Wolff and Agatha Deken, who lived in France until 1795 when the invasion brought them back. The dominating member of this famous pair was Betje Wolff, daughter of a respectable, liberal middle-class family who had been seized when quite young by the great 18th-century thoughts of tolerance, human dignity and progress, and rejection of dogmatic authority; by the application of his innate Reason man has the chance to perfect himself. An impetuous, independent spirit that had led to a brief affair with an officer and had later languished in a humdrum marriage to a much older preacher found expression in Betje's talent with the pen. In 1782, 52 years after Justus van Effen began publishing his *Spectator* and after she had already been widowed, she published under her name and that of her constant companion Aagje Deken the novel *Sara Burgerhart.*

Betje has something to say to her fellow countrymen – though she pointedly dedicates the novel only to young ladies – and she has no intention whatever of giving them one more tired imitation of a French novel: on her title page she proudly writes *niet vertaald*, not translated, unfortunately a necessary reminder in her time. Every people has to have its own writers, she says in the dedication, and only a native member of a society can observe it right. It is time, then, for an original Dutch novel,

... een Roman, die berekent is voor den Meridiaan des Huisselyken levens. Wy schilderen u Nederlandsche karakters; menschen, die men in ons Vaderland werkelyk vindt. . . . Wy maken u bekent met uwe landgenoten.*

By her own admission we have someone who is about to adopt the role of the painter, faithfully reflecting the society as it sees itself but at the same time performing the higher function of distilling out its most cherished ideals. Betje has much too fine a feeling for the limits of narrative to think that she can encompass all of society, however, and so with a highly deceptive innocence she narrows down the problems to a single one: how to get a vivacious, bright and emotional but somewhat vain young lady into the hands of enlightened but cautious and affectionate older women who can pilot her into a safe harbor of matrimony. We have no need of the silly abductions and

---

* a novel which is aimed at the level of domestic life. We paint Dutch personages for you, people one really finds in our native land. . . . We make you acquainted with your fellow countrymen.

poisonings of French plots, she assures us, but will meet numerous good people, some who fall victim to little vices, and a few bad ones, all of them alive, the way people really are. But Betje would have betrayed her Holland upbringing if she had allowed all these people to expose themselves even fictionally to too much glaring exposure of their inner selves. She has recourse to the popular 18th-century epistolary style, which means that each character can present himself in comfort and at leisure – but, as Betje's talent makes it turn out, with unintended candor. This commitment to letters is something of a handicap to a modern reader in that it gives a slow, deliberate pace to a novel that has no real climax at all, and it is not until a number of the characters have been introduced that we begin to sense the color and contour of the large canvas on which Betje is working. But our patience is well rewarded.

Sara Burgerhart is an orphan who lives with her aunt Suzanna Hofland, a religious fanatic who allows the teen-age girl little freedom and makes her dress very plainly. Sara soon rebels against this and goes to live in the home of the widow mevr. Spilgoed-Buigzaam. Most of this part of the story comes out in letters exchanged between Sara and her friends Aletta Brunier and Anna Willis. She also secures permission from her guardian Abraham Blankaart, a tolerant and enlightened man of strong opinions who writes a severe letter to Suzanna; her narrow-minded comrade Benjamin Slimpslamp writes a furious letter in reply to Blankaart, who however demolishes him with ease and elegance. The stage now having been set, we find Sara's life is an agreeable one if somewhat given to excessive vanity. She meets a number of young men in her new home: Jakob Brunier, whom she imperiously declines to take at all seriously, the staid Willem Willis – both of these the brothers of her friends – and the more forceful Hendrik Edeling, whose intentions with respect to Sara turn quite serious. This is then the crucial juncture at which Sara's somewhat scatterbrained lack of experience needs some guidance. The widow Spilgoed is kind but a bit too lax; Anna Willis, Sara's main confidante, is inclined to be priggishly self-righteous and has a temporary falling-out with Sara; her other friend Aletta is even more flighty than Sara herself. The Willis children's mother, another widow, is a model blend of affection and common sense, and has the best interests at heart not only of her son, whom she knows to be too mild-mannered to keep Sara's spirits properly in check, but also of Sara, whom she advises like a daughter. She and Blankaart both approve of the ripening relationship between Sara and Hendrik.

Here the plot, in so far as there is one at all, slows down for a time as further letters present discussions of morals and religion, talk about parties and dinners, shops and clothes, and continue drawing old and new characters more fully. Some of these are Cornelia Slimpslamp, who like her vindictive brother Benjamin and Suzanna Hofland can find little good in Sara, mej. Hartog, a disorganized, free-thinking femme savante, and mej. Doorzicht, a lady of genuine religious piety. We soon discover that Hendrik's Lutheran father is opposed to his son's projected marriage to someone brought up in the state religion, but Abraham Blankaart — who himself has little time for Catholicism — convinces him that toleration is in order. A while back Sara had become acquainted with a man known only as R., who in letters to a friend makes no secret of his dishonorable intentions but who manages to turn Sara's head. She is seen with him, prompting mej. Hartog to write Blankaart an anonymous letter accusing Sara of misconduct, and then it comes out that Sara had had a narrow escape from him: he had set the stage for a seduction at a farmhouse but an unforeseen circumstance at a critical moment had demanded his attention and allowed Sara to escape. This whole tale comes out in a letter, as do all others, but in a dialog form which heightens the vividness. Hendrik accepts her word that she is innocent, the two are married and eventually their first child is born. Following the 18th-century custom, a brief epilog assures us of the expected 'happily ever after' — Sara and Hendrik Edeling by now have five children — and outlines the further fate of the other important characters.

The bare plot is thus rather trivial, scarcely the sort of thing that can lay claim to immortality. What is missing in such a summary is the leisurely and elaborate interweaving of all these personalities in a multi-faceted picture of a living society. Though the characters inevitably strike the modern reader as a bit formalized and stylized in their stiffly regulated interaction with each other – even the rapturous letters Hendrik Edeling writes to his brother are couched in elegant, mannered terms –, they emerge as distinct and many-sided human beings. The polite and slightly reserved distance they maintain with respect to each other, clearly symbolized by their all communicating in letters, is itself a reflection of an established social game in which all feel comfortable and which all honor unquestioningly. Though they are very different sorts of people who often come into radical disagreement with each other, the smooth and uninterrupted flow of epistolary communication symbolizes their mutual participation in the game. It is noticeable that none of these people are Catholic, foreign, or members of the lower classes. The one exception to this, the nursemaid Pieternelletje, is treated with affection but also with a condescension that places her outside the game. The social interactions that emerge in these letters show plainly that the privileged middle class in Holland has changed very little over many centuries: it is self-sufficient and holds fast to a sober bourgeois standard of virtue, it tends strongly toward a practical, optimistic view of life, it places great weight on behavior that brings approval by one's neighbors and on accepting equally the role of approver, and above all it finds a perfect codification of all this in its religion, now permeated with the Age of Reason's confidence in right and progress.

But it would be a pity to content ourselves with having found a document on 18th-century manners and morals, however cleverly presented, when Betje Wolff and Aagje Deken give us plain hints that they mean for us to find more than this in their work. Their opening dedication to *Nederlandsche Juffers* contains at least two of these: first, the work was 'not translated' but written originally in Dutch, suggesting that the reader's native control of the language is to be called upon in a significant way; second, the actual happenings in the story are deliberately played down, subordinated to the sheer pleasure to be derived from the depiction itself – and of the fact that the authors are delighted by pure observation and deft characterization of people there can be no room for doubt. All this is put into focus with the familiar Dutch word *schilderen,* inviting the reader to notice that the authors are in fact setting out to paint with words, drawing on the many subtle potentialities of the native vernacular to brush in their multicolored canvas. And they make good on this promise. The reader with a perceptive ear soon discovers that each of the more than 20 important characters has his own distinct style in which he lives and presents himself just as in a painting each person is characterized by his taste and preference in dress and appearance. Sara writes effusively and impetuously, Abraham Blankaart's letters are unvaryingly whimsical and bluntly opinionated, filled with forceful descriptive adjectives, Willem Willis writes letters that are painfully and boringly correct, the Slimpslamps are slap-dash and crude, Pieternelletje's one or two notes are touching in their uneducated style full of colloquial mistakes. But for duller readers who may miss the point, names often hint heavily at character: mej. *Doorzicht* has a transparent clarity of vision, the minister *Redelijk* is a man of reason, mevr. Spilgoed née *Buigzaam* is flexible, perhaps a bit too much so, Pieternelletje *Degelijk* is solid and capable, and surely no knowledge of Dutch is required to hear the low character of the *Slimpslamps.* Hendrik *Edeling* is noble and is destined to help mold Sara's character in this direction, Sara herself represents a *Burger-hart,* the very embodiment of a middle-class ideal, and Abraham *Blankaart's* character is *blank* in the Dutch sense, enlightened, restrained on the moral level and above all taints of pettiness.

Watching a group of people playing a Dutch social game which is presented to us in a uniquely Dutch way inherited from prose writers such as Van Effen and the painters in equal measure, it dawns on us that all this is not just a period piece but yet another cultural myth. Sara Burgerhart is the Romantic side of the national character, given to sentiment and feeling but dangerously undisciplined and unable to

find her own way unaided. In the classic way of the *Bildungsroman*
she becomes, on being orphaned, the ward of Abraham Blankaart, the
intensely typical Hollander who embodies all the aspects of the other
side of the national character: he is bluff, tolerant, well-educated and
mature; he is a rich businessman with wide knowledge of the world
but with the Hollander's lack of sympathy for foreign ways, even in
Paris preferring to dine at a center where his compatriots congregate.
His mirroring of cultural ideals is complemented and supplemented by
the other main contributors to Sara's guidance: the widows Spilgoed
and Willis and, not by any means in the last place, the balanced,
urbane and intelligent Hendrik Edeling. But it is only when within the
established social game the two sides of an ideal character are fused
into one that the higher synthesis is achieved, the marriage of Sara
that is the goal of the narrative and that is the ultimate myth told by
Wolff and Deken. There are undoubtedly good autobiographical reasons why a story told by a widow and a spinster should be so
strikingly lacking in any normal warm family relationships — the
important women characters are all too young to marry, old maids or
widows, and Blankaart is a confirmed bachelor —'but artistically it is a
stroke of genius: no family preoccupations are allowed to distract our
attention from the wider claim of social interactions through which
the crucial synthesis comes about. As soon as Sara and Hendrik are
safely married, the authors lose all interest in them, and their five
children are relegated to the epilog.

It is a Dutch charade that is being acted out in Sara Burgerhart, a
myth told to Holland in the form of a Rationalistic mirror held up to
it. But it transcends these narrow limitations and rises to the level of a
work of art not only in the way the Dutch middle-class citizens
assume the dimensions of mythical prototypes, but even more in the
unity achieved between this mythological aim and Wolff and Deken's
exquisite control of the language.With an unfailing sense of how
society lives embedded in the language styles it creates, they reflect
and criticize the society by letting it speak for itself with its own
characteristic means. Through all the interaction of the persons in the

novel we feel the superior, ironic humor of the authors that retains just enough distance from the actors on the stage that we do not quite completely forget that ultimately they are all engaged in playing roles. For a worthy equal to this brilliant display of gentle and sophisticated irony we have to go back as far as the *Praise of Folly* and the *Colloquies* of Erasmus. Apparently none of his lessons have been forgotten.

12 Mid-afternoon: Camera Obscura

Though the tired Republic collapsed when prodded by the French and the once powerful, semi-autonomous East Indies Company came to an equally ignominious end soon after, and though voices were raised loudly as the Patriots assumed power, as a matter of fact the transition was made with a distinctly unrevolutionary order and lack of violence. Unlike France, where a new class was ready to take power on the dissolution of the old regime, here power was absorbed by the same middle class that had always exercised it through the instrumentality of the Regents. To be sure the old Regents were swept out of power and many of the Patriots were from social levels far removed from real affluence, but this whole middle class was so thoroughly formed by Regent culture that the influx of French Enlightenment ideals it had been absorbing merely had the effect of giving its traditional social ideals a fresh and even stronger foundation. Thus the dominant class itself is not by any means at an end but at its peak, and the 'noontime' metaphor is an entirely appropriate one.

The Netherlands now found that even with the Patriots in control, the ties with France were so close as to be almost suffocating. Under the regency of Rutger Jan Schimmelpenninck a number of progressive changes were made that formed the structure of the state more and more according to the French model. It was now called the Batavian Republic, a completely centralized structure in which the previously sovereign provinces were demoted to departments and the people were represented in an overall National Assembly, the old tax system was replaced and the Reformed Church was separated from the state and reduced to equality with all other churches. But during all this time the economy stagnated as the French cut off all trade and did their best to choke off the large-scale smuggling operations with England. When Napoleon became emperor in 1804 the French-style republic was incorporated even more absolutely into France, a process which was completed when in 1806 Napoleon replaced Schimmel-penninck with his brother Louis Napoleon. The new king did his best to continue progressive reforms in the country even to the point of occasionally running afoul of his brother's wishes, but in spite of the transformation of the state all the way from the legal system down to the institution of formal surnames, public apathy was more than he was able to overcome. Disillusionment at the extent of French control had set in early, but the reasons why the new reforms did not take permanent hold probably go deeper than this: according to Romein, the matter was simply that the Dutch people in all this period were never really presented with enough of a challenge to unite them in a meaningful response[1]; there was still a large prosperous class, and repression of other classes had never reached the critical proportions it had in other countries that produced genuine revolutionary movements. The Dutch of this time allowed the French to completely dominate them, and even when this domination was not in their interest they took little initiative in throwing it off. This came after Napoleon's defeat in 1812, when the victors drove out the French in the following year. A modest amount of Orange support was rallied, and Prince William, the son of William V who had died in exile, was made sovereign. In 1814 the Congress of Vienna, convened to redraw the map of Europe in the aftermath of Napoleon, reunited after nearly two and a half centuries the Northern and Southern Nether-lands into a single kingdom under the Orange successor, now known as William I. The history of the next fifteen years in one of continu-ous friction and discontentment on both sides. The North and the South had grown farther apart in the intervening centuries than people had suspected; the conservatively Catholic and economically backward South with a population of well over 3,000,000 now found itself strongly dominated by some 2,000,000 prosperous but arrogant heretics in the North, a feeling which led to resistance to the reforms attempted by the North. By 1830 violence had broken out in the South, and although warfare continued until the cease-fire in 1833, with French support Belgium declared its independence in 1831 and the two halves went their separate ways.

The curious circumstance has often been noted that the Netherlands finally culminated a very long development and became a monarchy under the House of Orange, the symbol of popular independence from domination by outside powers or domestic Regents, at the very point in the 19th century when everywhere else in Europe liberal movements were threatening the extinction of the outworn monarchic system. Everywhere, the changed economic conditions brought about by the industrial revolution produced massive unrest and attacks on the old systems of government that rested in the hands of the privileged. William I was authoritarian, a pure example of the old Regent paternalism, yet he was a liberal monarch who even without the antagonistic South had the impossible task of presiding over a chaotic and confused transition period leading from an old system to a modern one. Religious oppositions sharpened noticeably: the large Catholic minority largely concentrated in the traditionally ignored southern provinces, the old *generaliteitslanden* without equal rights, was less than ever willing to accept second-class status as a mere extension of Belgium, and in 1834 the whole conservative wing of the Reformed Church split off and became independent from the old *Hervormde Kerk*. Both the Catholic and the conservative Reformed groups were predominantly lower-class people who throughout the century were engaged in a struggle for equality. There was also unrest in the Indies, forfeited to England in the Napoleonic period but returned by the Congress of Vienna. In 1840, in the middle of still disordered times but with the new era on the way – a liberal constitution in 1848 was to put a final end to rule by the upper classes – William I grew tired of frustration and abdicated.

141

Mid-afternoon: Camera Obscura

In the midst of all this turbulence that was slowly transforming society from the bottom up, a good deal of life went on at a leisurely pace that was noticed by all of the Netherlands' contemporary neighbors. In 1839 Holland finally saw its first railroad line, running between Amsterdam and Haarlem, though not until after three years previously the States General itself had decided that national railroads were not necessary in a country with such an excellent system of water transport. In this same year, 57 years after the writing of *Sara Burgerhart,* there appeared under the name 'Hildebrand', the pen name of Nicolaas Beets, a work with the title *Camera Obscura.* The unparalleled popularity of this work − since it first appeared it has never been allowed to go out of print, and as this is being written it is in its 54th printing − makes it an obvious choice for our next pause.

In 1839 the 'camera obscura' was a contrivance in which a scene could be projected onto a piece of frosted glass and watched just as if the little figures were moving around inside the darkened box itself; only two years before, Daguerre had discovered how to give these projected scenes permanent form on a plate. It is just such a faithful reproduction of the colors and motions of an ordinary scene that Beets has in mind in his prefatory words:

De schaduwen en schimmen van Nadenken, Herinnering en Verbeelding vallen in de ziel als in eene Camera Obscura, en sommige zoo treffend en aardig dat men lust gevoelt ze na te teekenen en, met ze wat bij te werken, op te kleuren, en te groepeeren, er kleine schilderijen van te maken, die dan ook al naar de groote Tentoonstellingen kunnen gezonden worden, waar een klein hoekje goed genoeg voor hen is.*

---

* The shadows and shades of thought, recollection and imagination are projected in the soul like in a camera obscura, some of them so striking and pleasant that one feels an urge to copy them, and by touching them up, heightening the colors and grouping them, to make little paintings of them, which can then be sent to the great exhibitions, where a modest little corner is good enough for them.

142

This prepares the reader for exactly what he is to expect: a collection of modest miniatures whose only claim to unity is in the fact that they all despict different aspects of contemporary life. Several of them are barely three pages in length, but even the longest one, nearly· a hundred pages long, refuses to assume the proportions of a large canvas because the artist keeps his eye on the everyday and remains serenely undistracted by the troubled heights and depths of human nature. An example of this is *De familie Stastok*, one of the two longest sketches.

The retelling of a story like this sounds just about as lame as the verbal description of an engraving or painting; it is the variety of sights and sounds experienced by our humble servant Hildebrand and set down for us that counts. Hildebrand arrives one fine October day by carriage in D – , and immediately demonstrates that he has wasted no time during the ride when he deftly types and places all the people who shared the journey with him. He has come to visit the Stastoks, whose son Pieter has been sent to the station to meet the guest but who in a fit of eccentric bashfulness manages to miss him. The meeting with the family is naturally the occasion for penetrating observation of all their little peculiarities and habits, and they immediately begin typing themselves by their use of favorite expressions. A tour of the town and a visit to a coffee house allow the personality of Pieter, the shy, clumsy but somewhat conceited student, to come to the foreground as the central figure around which the others are going to be grouped. An interlude now tells in vivid colors the story of the injustices suffered by an old man in a charity home, giving Hildebrand the chance for a tour de force in bringing lower-class accents into the story. The following scene gives Hildebrand's brush a free hand as he creates with loving attention every detail of the room in which an evening get-together with visitors is taking place. From the table with the objects on it he moves to the people, who in their polite interaction all find themselves exposed to Hildebrand's affectionate but unsparing gaze and whose idiosyncrasies are all recorded in pungent terms. In the course of the long evening it turns out that son Pieter has fallen for one of the young ladies present. To give Pieter a chance to make his feelings plainer a group of the younger generation goes out rowing the next day, but his attempts to make an impression collapse when he manages to fall into the water. The day after this the time comes for Hildebrand to depart, with Pieter's desperate problem still unsolved.

When we reach the end of this lengthy sketch we discover that it has not presented us with any plot at all, but instead we are left with a feeling of having stood in front of a static representation, scrutinizing it meticulously under the guidance of an expert who helps us penetrate much more deeply into it. Thanks to Beets' keen eye plus his ability *bij te werken, op te kleuren, en te groepeeren,* we have a very considerable feeling for the perfectly ordinary sized personality of Pieter as it emerges in the interaction with the members of his family, and for this family itself as a functioning social unit. Beets' deliberate focusing on the family as the immediate context within which one's social existence is embedded is relatively new to the literature – we noticed that half a century previously Wolff and Deken showed little direct interest in it – but it reflects an institution that was long occupied a central position in the system of cultural values. At least as far back as Jan Steen there is clear evidence that the family functioned as the fundamental social unit, a situation that is still just as true today; the social importance of the family has been given cultural formalization in a variety of interesting ways, not by any means the least of which is the strongly family-oriented celebration of *Sint Nicolaas* on the evening of December 5, in actuality a culture-wide birthday celebration and thus a ritual reminder of the family significance the culture assigns to the birthday.[2] In the two long sketches that occupy a central position in the Camera Obscura, Beets chooses the family as the frame within which meaningful human interactions take place, and it is not entirely inappropriate that in the second of these two, the longest of the whole collection, an oblique reminder of the *Sint Nicolaas* custom stands right in the center.

De familie Kegge did not appear in the 1839 edition but was added some years later. It has much less the quality of a tableau than the other large family sketch. Here Hildebrand meets William Kegge, a student from the Dutch West Indies who soon contracts typhus, and just before he dies gives Hildebrand a mysterious ring with the initials E. M. on it. Hildebrand writes the sad news to William's family, and when two years later they come to the Netherlands he immediately accepts an invitation to visit them. The father turns out to be an ebullient, good-hearted but vulgar parvenu who speaks in clichés and knows better ways of doing everything. The mother and the daughter Henriette are almost equally individualistic but just as lacking in any real cultivation. On succeeding visits Hildebrand meets more members of the Kegges' circle, for instance Henriette's cousin Saartje who arouses jealousy in her, and a certain Van der Hoogen, a shallow, pretentious young libertine who takes it into his head to begin pursuing Henriette. By this time Hildebrand has solved the puzzle of the ring entrusted to his keeping: it turns out to have been given to William not by someone whose heart he was cruelly torn away from but by. . . his grandmother! This serene old lady, known only as E. Marrison, is the most enlightened, human and down-to-earth of the whole cast of characters. In a chapter characteristically entitled *Om te bewijzen, dat eenvoudige genoegens ook genoegens zijn,** the unruffable Hildebrand volunteers to replace a petulant Henriette at a party of girls organized to decorate figures for the coming *Sint Nicolaas* celebration. Here he meets, among others, the grave Suzette Noiret, whose aging mother lives in a *hofje,* a type of charity establishment for the aged, and who is frightened by the prospect that her mother might die during the night when she could not get to her. This is followed, after another scene in which the grandmother's high regard for William is drawn more fully, by a lively charity concert at which Henriette makes a hit with her piano performance and funny but uncharitable judgements of the other participants are heard from the family. The sketch reaches a climax as our faithful Hildebrand rescues

* To prove that simple pleasures are also pleasures.

Mid-afternoon: Camera Obscura

Miss Noiret from the pestering of the cad Van der Hoogen and soon after discovers the baseness of his intentions with relation to Henriette. He boldly intervenes and forces him to reduce his attentions to the polite and reserved level. In the end all the strings are brought together: Van der Hoogen has left in a huff, the mother of Suzette Noiret had died peacefully in the presence of her daughter, the grandmother has died and given the ring back to Hildebrand, and Suzette, Saartje and Henriette are all safely married or engaged — none of them, to be sure, to the incorrigibly footloose spectator Hildebrand.

Here again, as in the case of Pieter Stastok, we watch on the frosted glass the lively movements of all the colorful people surrounding one completely ordinary personality, only here this family context which formed his social self is so dominant that he himself has been removed from the stage by the author before the description itself even begins, a touch equal to Wolff and Deken's device of showing us the creation of a new family by widows, spinsters and a bachelor. But by means of the ring, the link between William and the ethical ideal of the grandmother which was put directly into Hildebrand's hands, his presence is continually felt. Only William stands out in relief — if this is not mixing a metaphor — from the charming but essentially petty vanities of all the other characters.

The collection also contains *Gerrit Witse,* a sketch about a student and his family carried to considerable length but left unfinished, and a number of short pieces. These make no attempt to be other then miniatures, dealing with a single event or encounter, or some aspect of contemporary life such as water, exhibitions of paintings, funeral customs or the types of people in various regions of the country engaged in a wide variety of occupations. All of these vivid, colorful and imaginative pieces are arranged like a garland around the two large family sketches we looked at. Taken all together, the *Camera Obscura* offers us a picture of the very same class of people we have been watching for a long time, here neither the

146

exalted peaks of power nor the lowest reaches at which its culture was imitated. With his gentle but determined criticism Beets seems to be reflecting a conservative, untroubled culture that had found the only sensible way of doing things, and that was naturally unaware of the lengthening afternoon shadows cast by its privileged institutions.

So the question is, again, whether a writer has managed to do more than provide posterity with some quaint genre painting of a bygone era. Certainly anyone who set about claiming for Nicolaas Beets a place beside the great 19th-century novelists of other countries would struggle with a very heavy burden of proof: here the surface of existence is not pulled back to reveal the raw essentials of it, nobody performs an act that ennobles humanity, and personalities are not larger than life. If Beets has his own kind of immortality, it lies quite simply in his having looked with a special kind of perception at all of ordinary life and in some way heightened contour, color and grouping until it all assumed proportions that are larger than life. He becomes for a moment the culture's observer, its spectator, in the same way in which Vermeer and Van Eyck were centuries back, and like them he finds a transcendent dimension of mysterious luminescence in all the most familiar, ordinary things. If a true universal greatness cannot be claimed for him it is because his horizons were too modestly limited to those of his mid-afternoon culture with its resolute blindness to the terrifying or awe-inspiring, and not because of any inherent smallness in his knowledge that true seeing involves unsuspected depths of humanity and a compassionate ability to perceive persons and things in all their uniqueness. Beets thus sees with the eyes of Van Eyck and Vermeer, but with a mid-19th century light that makes the individual figures stand out with a modern three-dimensionality. Not as isolated individuals but as meaningful components in a setting.

Like the best observers, Beets does not take himself overly seriously. With his playful, ironic manipulation of an elegant language he is not above poking a little fun at his ever busy alter ego Hildebrand joining in the often frantic movement of the little figures on the frosted glass.

147

In fact Beets did not even take the *Camera Obscura* itself with what he considered undue seriousness, and many have wondered why someone who produced a popular and successful masterpiece such as this at a relatively young age never showed the slightest interest in producing other works of the same kind. It is almost as if Beets himself, who regarded his ultra-serious and proper career as a preacher as his real life's work, did not fully appreciate the role humor plays in greatness, or the extent to which his own Dutch instinct for irony was a vital ingredient in his immortality. One wonders whether he had pondered all the implications of the epigram of Horace's with which he offers us his *Camera Obscura:*

Nec lusisse pudet, sed non incidere ludum,

which can be rendered very freely as something like 'There is no disgrace in having played, but only in never bringing the game to an end.'

13 Evening: Small Souls

Het stortregende en Dorine van Lowe was doodmoe, toen zij, die middag, vóór het diner nog even bij Karel en Cateau aanwipte, maar Dorine was tevreden over zichzelf. Zij was na de lunch dadelijk uitgegaan en had heel Den Haag doortrippeld en doortramd. . . *

With these words Louis Couperus opened at the turn of the century his novel *De boeken der kleine zielen*.[1] They put us in The Hague, the offical administrative center of Holland and therefore of the Netherlands. Couperus had a first-hand familiarity with the society of his native city, and not only did his long residence abroad sharpen his penetrating observation into an almost painfully acute awareness of its inner workings, but the fact that most of these years were spent in Indonesia and the Mediterranean — this novel was written in Nice — provided him in a natural way with a heightened sense of the artistic importance of the setting. The rain into which we are plunged by the first two words, the chilly autumn wind and the damp, somber air of Ruysdael run like a leitmotiv throughout this long novel, constantly hanging over the doings of a rigidly-structured little microcosm now at the end of its days and fully aware of this: the upper-crust society of The Hague in the closing years of the 19th century and the first decades of the 20th. The unnatural, distinctly *précieux* tone of this

* It was pouring rain and Dorine van Lowe was dead tired when, that afternoon, just before dinner she dropped in for a minute at Karel and Cateau's, but Dorine was pleased with herself. She had gone out right after lunch and had been tripping and trolleying all over The Hague.

same first sentence is, like every sentence in all of Couperus' volumi-
nous works, a reminder of the instantly recognizable style he made
uniquely his own as a means of interposing a sort of screen between
the observer and his subject, a signal of the artist's indispensable
perspective on it.

The Van Lowes are one of a small number of proud old families, the
last unadulterated remnants of the Regent class who like their ancestors have devoted themselves primarily to government service at home
and in the Indies. Papa Van Lowe had served, until his death a few
years ago, as Governor General of the Netherlands East Indies, where
most of his family was born and raised. Now the Van Lowe family all
lives in The Hague, and although some of its members are still active
in government and diplomatic service, it devotes most of its affluent
leisure to basking in the glory of the fading past and determinedly
carrying on increasingly empty social rituals with its equals, other
families with the 'proper' credentials. Under the somber skies of
Holland the traditional enlightened tolerance of this class has
degenerated into a rigid exclusion of all who do not fit, and its
long-standing middle-class interest in the behavior of others has now
solidified into a blind preoccupation with the 'proper' image in which
all are thoroughly ensnared. So intensely real is Couperus' evocation
of a narrow-minded, stiff-necked society playing a wistful game in the
long evening shadows and giving a whole city a tone that has yet to
wear off, that many Dutch readers of an older generation still find it
impossible to read him with the necessary detachment.

The extensive and complex Van Lowe family has, for all its frictions
and centrifugal tendencies, a deeply ingrained instinct for family
solidarity which is ritually sanctified by the benign Mama Van Lowe
in weekly Sunday-evening get-togethers at her home. Daughter
Dorine's frantic activity is in preparation for one of these, but a very
special one that has everybody's nerves on edge: Constance, another
of Mama's children, has been abroad for many years and is now about
to return to the fold. When she was hardly out of her teens she had

been married to a considerably older diplomat, and while they were living in Rome she had rashly gotten involved in an affair with an official younger than herself. The scandal of course threw all three of the intensely proud families involved into a turmoil, which subsided somewhat when the young Van der Welcke yielded to his parents' pressure and married Constance, a step which ruined his promising diplomatic career and did little to reconcile Constance's family to the blemish inflicted on their name. It was generally believed in the family, though seldom mentioned, that Papa Van Lowe's death had actually been of remorse over this act. Constance and Van der Welcke continued to live abroad, isolated from their families and with the bleak realization that they were not really compatible with each other, but held together by their son Addy. Now Constance is over 40, tired of all this, and desires nothing but to return to Holland and be accepted once again into the family where she belongs. Though she is fully conscious of the seriousness of her past actions and accepts all responsibility for them, she fatally underestimates the strength of the social rules working in a direction opposite to her wish: her family's very existence depends on its playing strictly by these rules, and they decree that no violation of the accepted moral standards may be tolerated. The central conflict of Couperus' novel is thus the one between one's natural affection for a family member and the powerful demands imposed by one's social identity, and a large share of the family's present anger is resentment at being forced to make this very choice.

The novel consists of four books, the first of which is called *De kleine zielen*. At the long-awaited Sunday party we are not only introduced to the entire family but become sharply aware, through conversations and stream-of-consciousness presentation, of the great latent reservoirs of both attachment and hostility in all of them. The rather pale and self-effacing Dorine we have already met; Adolfine, the third sister, is married to Van Saetzema, a minor government official who never rose to the brilliant heights she would so dearly love; she is abrasive and spends her days in bitterness and frustration, intensely jealous of the attractive, poised Constance and of her successful and socially prominent older sister Bertha. Bertha is married to Van Naghel, the present head of the Ministry of Colonies. She is mature and has a warm affection for Constance, but her exalted social position leaves her even less room for individual social preferences than is true of the others. Of the four sons, Karel is a former mayor now retired and vegetating with his wife Cateau in a rigidly formalized, self-indulgent and pointless life. Gerrit is a large, hearty blond cavalry officer, naively proud of his strength and vitality and of the large family his wife Adeline has presented him with. Paul is a cynical bachelor whose passion for cleanliness and order borders on the neurotic, but whose sharp criticism of the smallness he sees around him and whose deep loyalty to Constance show a clarity of vision the others lack. Ernst, the last brother, is a morose recluse who lives in a shadowy fantasy world of his own that reflects in its own way his perception of much that is wrong. Notwithstanding the understanding and acceptance Constance finds in many members of her family, the first book shows her determined humility wearing thin and the tensions generated by her return gradually building toward a crisis. In an atmosphere of continual thin-skinned overreaction and backbiting – which Constance herself is not free from, inasmuch as she and Van der Welcke can communicate and cooperate only via the mediation of the solemn child Addy – all the brothers and sisters are driven to extreme positions from which it is difficult to retreat. Constance's attempts at reconciliation are interpreted as undue social aggressiveness, her painstakingly nurtured relationship with her difficult sister Adolfine collapses in a disastrous outburst of pent-up emotions that nearly brings about a duel, and even relations with the motherly oldest sister Bertha are strained to the breaking point when Constance shows up uninvited at one of her exclusive receptions. Constance is forced to fall back in despair before what looks like a solid phalanx of small souls.

In contrast to the breathless onrush of events in the first book, *Het late leven* is much more reflective. It is not as if there were not a

considerable dose of action here too: Bertha's daughter Emilie is torn
out of an unusually close and loyal attachment among her siblings and
married to a dull young man who hardly matches her in spirit, and
when before long she leaves him there in an emotional scene at the
Van Naghel home that ends with a somewhat theatrical stroke that
kills the father. The immature Van der Welcke has found a wholly
innocent but faintly scandalous relationship with his niece, once again
illustrating the inability of this entire family to find any real meaning
in what might be called a 'normal' love relationship between two
persons. But the real theme of this book is, as before, Constance's
adjustment to the situation she finds herself confronted with. Much of
the dust has settled, she has continued maturing, and her life is given a
new direction with the advent of Max Brauws, an old acquaintance
who has now made it his mission to spread the ideas on peace and
social justice held by the still relatively new Socialist movement.
Constance is not ready for most of the radical ideas, but the relationship of profound understanding that develops between her and
Brauws makes possible a quiet resignation and an abiljty to create her
own moral ground above the petty world of her family.

In the third book, *Zielenschemering,* Constance recedes somewhat to
the background while all the time she ripens into a source of comfort
and support for her whole troubled family. First our attention is
drawn to the strange Ernst, who sinks into a psychopathic state that
creates tortured souls all around him that all trample on but he
himself, and who emerges from this only in response to some strange
power that Addy is able to exercise over him. Addy does not quite
understand this either, but resolves to devote himself to its cultivation. This book, however, really belongs to the husky, uncomplicated
Cavalry officer Gerrit. Gerrit is not so simple after all. His jovial
optimism is nothing but a front concealing a troubled soul who is in
despair over the weakness and mortality he finds so terrifyingly close
to the surface, like a worm inside somewhere constantly gnawing his
life away from the inside. When Pauline, an old acquaintance with
whom he had had a questionable relationship some years before,

arrives in town, a storm of guilt feelings forces Gerrit to reexamine his relations to everyone, especially his wife and children, and all the inner workings of his tormented mind are exposed to an extent that is nearly overwhelming. All this comes to a climax in a long, surrealistic chapter that purely in terms of a tour de force surely has no superior in any literature: a tired and feverish Gerrit wanders about the streets of The Hague, troubled by the news that Emilie's brother Henri, with whom she had been living in Paris, had just been murdered, by the disappearance of Pauline at the same time when Constance has left for Paris to bring back the body, and by the report that a woman's body has just been found in one of the canals. In his disordered mind the gnawing worm now emerges, becomes thoroughly entangled with his worries, and eventually fills the sky in front of him, the dragon of his own weakness and guilt. With all the persons and events thoroughly confused in his mind he collapses at home with typhoid fever, later recovers but, when he discovers himself completely hollowed out inside, commits suicide.

The fourth book, *Het heilige weten,* is devoted mainly to the ethical development of Addy. It is now ten years later, and the scene is again relatively restful and reflective as in the second book. Addy has fulfilled his ideal and become a doctor working with underprivileged people, and the family is now living in Driebergen, far from The Hague but still very much in its shadow. Addy's healing power also extends to the family: Ernst is still under his care, Adolfine is forced to swallow her pride and ask for help for her precariously balanced daughter Marietje, and it is only to Addy that Emilie dares confide the truth that her brother Henri's murder in Paris had been at the hands of her estranged husband. All Addy's precocious wisdom has not prevented him from choosing very much the wrong kind of wife, and the souls become small again until Mathilde demands that he take her and the two children back to The Hague where her naive vanity can have freer rein. Here Addy's suspicions about himself are realized as he finds he has grown away from her and must respond to the *heilig weten* stirring in himself. He travels for three months to come to

154

terms with things, and arrives back in Driebergen only shortly before
Mama Van Lowe, the last reminder of the old order who by now has
lapsed into senility, dies quietly in her sleep.

This summary may seem overly long, but even so it gives practically
no hint of the epic scope of this family portrait and even less of the
constant, vibrant interaction among all the constantly changing personalities in the story. They are all exquisitely real, with all the
unpredictable complexity of real-life motivation that emerges in conversation, stream of thoughts, or the author's description. But at the
same time they are all too predictable in their imprisonment in a
social setting from which none of them can hope to escape. There is
not one character in the novel, with the exception of Mama Van Lowe
and her two absurd, deaf old sisters, who does not really want to be
free from this morally suffocating society, though most of them are
totally unaware of this. Directly or indirictly this underlying urge
haunts Bertha as she realizes the futility of her frantic existence, keeps
Paul in a constant misanthropic state, propels Ernst into insanity,
reduces Adolfine to a bitter shadow of a person, makes Dorine and
Karel vegetables respected by nobody and kills Gerrit. All the characters grow and change as they all react in their different ways to this
underlying conflict, but it is only Constance and her son Addy who
are able to rise to a moral independence that makes possible an uneasy
truce. Many writers before Couperus have made central in their
thinking the importance of the social setting in forming the individual's existence; many others, who have been beyond our limited
horizons here, have criticized this social setting. But it remained for
Couperus to reduce this whole problem to its ultimate essentials:
What happens when the inborn moral dignity of the individual, the
uniqueness perceived by members of this culture at least as far back as
Geert Grote in the 14th century, comes into irreconcilable conflict
with the degrading demands of a decadent moral system thas has
congealed into an anxious dependence on the opinions of others?
This is a universal problem, but it appears here in an unmistakably
Dutch form in the mind of a writer whose first-hand familiarity with

other cultures focused the central problem of his own. He did not provide any obvious answer, certainly not an outright rejection and rebellion. Rather he seems to finish by saying that, as all his cultural ancestors have perceived, it is impossible to be an individual in a truly meaningful sense outside of the social interactions that create his individuality and give it its field of application. We seem to be left, then, with the obligation to undertake a mighty struggle to find the significant, acceptable dimensions even in a social system that is not directed toward nourishing human individuality, the carving out of a humanly meaningful life under the heavy skies that cannot really be escaped from. Constance and Addy show us that the ultimate victory is not a bold transformation of society but a serenely resigned life of creative response to the immediate environment. Mama Van Lowe dies, already hopelessly out of touch with the world of the present, but Brauws also fades out of the picture again. The entire family looks toward Constance and Addy, who have made their peace and grow on into the future, each with their own brand of *heilig weten.*

But for all the sharpness of focus on a very real problem that gives Couperus' work a stature far transcending the narrow borders of his country, the little self-reflecting microcosm he immortalized was already being bypassed as he wrote just as surely as the self-assured Burgundian knightly culture was doomed to be overtaken by the stirrings of the Renaissance. In the 63 years that elapsed between the mellow confidence of the *Camera Obscura* and the forlorn resignation of *De boeken der kleine zielen* in 1902, the mainstream of the society was faced with new challenges and continued to evolve vigorous new responses. This mainstream was, as always, the prosperous bourgeoisie, the broad middle class whose anti-Regent, liberal orientation goes back at least to the Patriots, the 18th-century heirs to the Enlightenment. The gradual shift of power from the hands of the old Regent elite to an increasingly broadening segment of the society reached a climax in the second half of the 19th century and resulted within a few decades in a complete reorientation of the political spectrum of the country. This liberal *burgerij* with an enlightened system of thought disseminated by people like Beets held a high ideal of social democracy, which on the surface looks like the true heritage of the best days of the old Republic. It was given articulate form by a mid-century group of intellectuals, most conspicuously in a crusading literary magazine called *De Gids* – 'the Guide', a title that unintentionally betrays a not entirely unprecedented instinct for moralizing.

From the vantage point of a century it is not overly difficult to see a certain discrepancy between enlightened social outlook and hard reality. This class was playing every bit as much of a social game as was the class of Couperus in its late evening; one of the cardinal rules in this game was a careful concealment of the fact that there were other social classes whose right to equality may have been a specifically espoused social ideal but who should not be presumptuous enough to break down class differences too rapidly or too soon. Every game, by virtue of the fact that its essence is a set of rules assented to by its participants, casts a spell and is therefore always vulnerable to the player who chooses to break the spell. The spellbreaker of this mid-19th-century social game was an author who called himself simply Multatuli, 'I have borne much', and who in 1860 wrote a remarkable novel called *Max Havelaar.*[2] On the surface this work is an impassioned indictment of the Dutch government's oppressive exploitation of its empire in the Indies, and analysis of it would take us too far afield here. By means of a highly sophisticated stylistic tour de force, Multatuli reflects himself autobiographically in several characters at the same time, and thereby sets up a dialectic through which the reader experiences Max Havelaar's outrage in the colonies but at the same time feels the full weight of the paternalistic hypocrisy back home that supports this brutal exploitation. With a mixture of earnestness and caricature Multatuli leads the reader outside the social game, shows him the breadth of its pretense, and for the first time summons him to direct responsibility for its rules.

Multatuli's concern did not stop with the plight of the far-off peoples in the colonies, but he attempted as well to speak directly to *het volk,* the less privileged levels of society who were still standing on the fringes of its dominant culture. By the second half of the century these groups, mainly the Catholic and conservative Protestant *kleine burgerij,* developed a sufficiently strong class consciousness that they were able to form together a third distinct bloc and accelerate political changes. At the same time as the large liberal middle bloc was tending more and more to allow its religious outlook to drift off into irrelevancy to everyday social life, the less privileged class found precisely in its strong confessional orientation the means for the gaining of equality on all levels. Down on this level the Catholics on the one hand and the Protestants on the other – we have already noted the *Afscheiding* from the Reformed Church in 1834, an event that was repeated in 1886 to bring into being the *Christelijk Gereformeerde Kerk* – refurbished the ancient concept of 'privilege' and fought for separate-but-equal churches, schools, social organizations and political parties. In this protective gathering of a variety of social concerns under a single unifying *levensbeschouwing,* a gradual and wholly natural development of the social structure of the Netherlands, we witness the real birth of modern *verzuiling.* This 19th-century development had two effects on the large middle bloc; either it had to reverse its trend away from confessional ties and identify itself in self-defense with liberal Protestantism, which to a considerable extent it did, or it had to go all the way and dissolve the ties completely, finding its political unity elsewhere. The liberal political faith that spoke most strongly to this modest but growing bloc of what is today called *buitenkerkelijken* – not all of them from the liberal middle group – was Socialism. This is not the place to review the history of the important role played by 19th- and 20th-century Socialism in Netherlands society, or to discuss the many important literary figures who were inspired by its ideals. What is most significant is that a general European social and political ideal was imported much as Calvinism had been three centuries before, and like it was transformed into a fresh expression of cultural rules of long standing. Socialism expressed again the instinct for tolerance and the free exercise of initiative toward practical progress; it became a non-confessional *levensbeschouwing* to which many were committed, and it took its place, as we saw in the second chapter, in the unique cultural invention known as *verzuiling.*

Social change that is really significant in scope is inevitably attended by abrasion and the release of destructive forces that threaten the cohesion, or even the continued survival, of the society. This was true of the restless 19th century to an extent that was the despair of many contemporary observers. But what strikes us now in all this rapid social transformation is the very smoothness with which the society of the Netherlands again, as at previous times in its history, absorbed potentially destructive revolutionary energy. The answer to the question of how this happened seems to lie in the remarkable strength of the middle-class ethic that was born in the prosperous Medieval cities and brought to maturity by the culture of the Regents. Centuries of suspicion and hatred of the arrogant Regents did not stand in the way of a large-scale imitation of their ways of life, and this way of life became such a thoroughly appropriate cultural expression that even the rebellion of the lower classes did not result in a break with the culture of the oppressing classes but an almost complete absorption into it. While it would be somewhat absurd to claim that some six centuries of social change in the Netherlands can be seen as a continuous demand by the 'out' groups for the right to share in the game played by the 'in', this is not without a certain small element of truth.

Those of us privileged to observe the functioning of a constitutional monarchy but not brought up in one may be pardoned for fancying that we can detect particular significance in the role assigned by the culture of the Netherlands to its monarchs. If we lower our sights from the austere level of government and military enterprise for a few moments, the way in which the originally alien House of Orange has through the centuries become a cultural symbol is striking indeed. In the 16th and 17th centuries William of Orange, his son Maurits and their successors were not only the indispensable military defenders of the Netherlands but the symbols of the preservation of its traditional, 'privileged' way of life; in the era of increasing alienation between the small Regent group and the large common group it was the name of Orange that symbolized popular loyalty to the cultural ideals of universal tolerance the Regents were believed to have abandoned, and the steady eclipse of Orange through most of the 18th century was the result of their having failed to sense the changing mood of the society that found its underlying identity better symbolized by the French Enlightenment. Throughout these centuries the symbolic importance of Orange was its role of leadership of those who were absorbing and consolidating an urban culture: William's main support came from the cities. In restoring the Orange dynasty as head of the state, now as kings rather than as stadhouders, the Congress of Vienna acted with a cultural insight that was surely unintentional. Its resumption of power after the Napoleonic period was shaky, but throughout the 19th century a very interesting development took place: at the same time that a constitutional form of government was being strengthened and liberalized, meaning that the leadership of the state and that of its government were diverging more and more, the popularity of the Orange kings steadily increased. The striking fact has already been noted that the Netherlands acquired a monarch just at the point where most other societies were ridding themselves of theirs, but this circumstance becomes distinctly more logical when we perceive that the creation of the monarchy was, on the cultural level, the natural culmination of a very long development. Throughout its history Netherlands society has been a precarious collection of equals, and it has always needed a symbolic – and often a very real – guarantor of the preservation of this balance. But at still another level, the society evolved an elaborate and remarkably stable and homogeneous cultural game as its symbolism, the system of moral standards and accepted ways in which 'things are done', and an esteemed royal family was a visible reminder of the social constraints of reserve and polite distance that applied to all participants in the culture. The adherence of wider and wider segments of the population to the rules of this particular game, and the readiness on the part of 'outsiders' to

160

participate in it, at least partly explains the strength of popular support of the monarchy during the 19th century, precisely the time in which the game became more nearly universal than ever before. Today the constitutional monarch is a symbol — whatever other important functions she may have, and widespread republican sentiment notwithstanding — with close analogies to the cultural role of the Dukes of Burgundy: a permanently visible participant in the game, the keystone where all its social rules of proper behavior come together. Everyone's social relations are a mixture, in unequal measure, of politeness and intimacy, but all are absolutely equal, from the top of society to the bottom, in their obligation to address the monarch in her capacity as such — even if it is only a theoretical obligation for the majority of people — with a polite reserve. Thus, in a way that is not all obvious to someone not a member of the culture, the political function of a monarchy that stands above the potentially divisive *zuilen* and guarantees the rights of all blocs has been transformed at the symbolic level into a faithful mirror of the very cultural agreements that hold the system together: the preservation of a polite reserve and the participation in a system of uniform middle-class standards of behavior that includes moral approval and the maintenance of a certain acceptable image.

The most wholehearted support for the monarchy comes, however, not from the center of the middle class but rather from the top and the bottom. The royal family shows distinctly paternalistic traits, something we were able to discern as far back as William the Silent himself, and is now no longer in opposition to the Regent elite in its present-day form but completely merged with it and enthusiastically supported by it. But the dynasty's firm base of support in the lower levels of the middle class has also remained, the conservative segments of society that treasure stability, morality and order and have a strong belief in authority they see embodied in the monarchy. In its own mixture of bourgeois ordinariness and regal aloofness, the present royal family shows an instinctive grasp of its symbolic role, and even its lapses have tended to prove the reality of this symbolism. More than once in recent years events involving the royal family have generated popular disapproval and resulted in an increase in anti-royalist sentiment. But the conspicuous demonstrations that have attended one or two solemn ceremonial functions were recognized by the population at large not as attacks on persons or on a constitutional provision but, with the infallible instinct of a culture for the underlying meaning of its own symbols, as the rebellion of a younger generation against the constraints imposed by the society itself.

14 Contemporary challenges

When the word 'challenge' is applied to a culture or a society it usually refers to the fact that in order to remain a viable institution it must continually and creatively take account of changing circumstances or environment. But a challenge may equally well come from within, as when certain members withdraw their consent to some of the underlying rules or a single individual like Multatuli proclaims them to be wrong. We now find ourselves faced with the formidable task of discovering some of the principal formative rules of the culture of the Netherlands as it exists in the present day, and we saw in Chapter 2 that there are few more effective revelations of the rules than the disruptions and challenges that bring them out into the open. One final leap from the epic social novel of Couperus over the span of 62 years brings us to 1964, closing our circle with the same year with which we began. This year and the two following ones brought not only the *Zo is het* episode but two distinct challenges that are by now just far enough in the past that we can attempt a somewhat detached evaluation of their symbolic importance.

In February 1964, a society with its nerves still on edge in the aftermath of the *Zo is het* TV controversy was suddenly confronted with a paperback called simply *Ik Jan Cremer*.[1] The pros and cons of its purely literary merits were completely drowned out by the righteous indignation that arose on all sides and assured bestseller status to a book that with a grand disregard for the consequences proceeded to talk about everything that is was 'impolite' to talk about. There is scarcely a plot to summarize, because the book is little more than a rambling series of adventures, crude, shocking, hilarious or even tender, held together only by an attitude of bluster and swagger and an unfailing sense of vivid narration. In a culture that traditionally prescribes that its literature be couched in a somewhat austere and properly elegant style, this narrative never departs from the colloquial level and in fact flaunts a proletarian flavor by using elegant language inappropriately and spelling German, French and English words so as to suggest grotesque mispronunciations. But even a literary rebel setting out to break all the taboos is unable to escape from the culture's long-ingrained identification of writing and painting: the hero frequently boasts of his renown as a painter, and even though Cremer assures the reader that everything is invented, he does in fact seem to have dabbled in pop-art in real life.

Readers who are relatively immune to the shock that is dealt out by the surface narration sooner or later discover that they are in the hands of a picaresque hero in the grand manner of the 16th and 17th centuries, the rogue who in his boisterous chain of fights, daredevil exploits and conquests of women proclaims to society 'I'm not playing your game' and does everything that it itself really does but that it says it does not do. Like the hero of the classic picaresque novel, the modern hero of this one methodically lays about him with a stick and hits all the tender places where the society sets up the most inviolable taboos. The laughter is loudest precisely where the cultural game is at its most solemn, but the mirth is not so much cruel as it is liberating. All Dutch readers noticed before very long that the book contains literally every vulgarism and obscenity that the language has to offer and gives full play to the rich vocabulary of impolite society. The scandal it generated was a direct result of its challenging the elaborate means used by polite bourgeois society to tell itself what is 'right' and 'proper' for a person to do and not to do. In other words, by renouncing any suggestion of anxiety or hypocrisy about morals, it systematically replaces the ordinary, familiar vocabulary of morality with the anti-vocabulary that society keeps hidden, and thus creates an exact mirror image of the culture it represents. This intent is proclaimed unambiguously in the title *Ik Jan Cremer* itself. The first word begins the task of creating an outsized ego which instinctively places 'I' first in a culture in which one's individual self is meticulously hedged about with restrictions and safeguards. The very abrasiveness of this particular cultural myth suggests that we look for some of the rules it is challenging, particularly those that are verbal in nature.

We have had more than one occasion to note that when a person speaks he is engaging not primarily in an act of individual expression but in an intensely social act. Even if he chooses to mumble a purely private opinion out of anyone's hearing, he is thoroughly bound by social agreements to formalize feelings, things and events in certain ways. At a superficial level, the Dutch speaker's use of *u* or *jij* as forms of address is a social act of a simple sort carrying the implication that the person addressed is being held at a respectful distance or admitted to a degree of intimacy. The more deeply-embedded levels of a language also represent social acts, which can be illustrated by a simple example: the references of descriptive words such as 'wet', 'large', 'hungry', 'hot' and the like have been set by cultural habit, and all speakers, including the unheard one just mentioned, accept without question the many rules like these by which the culture makes easy communication possible. They are so natural that speakers are normally surprised to discover that other cultures may define something such as 'hot' in a much different way. But at still another level, an even more interesting one for our purposes, speaking a language is more than the expression of an opinion or communication with another speaker by means of a complicated system of social agreements; it is at the same time carrying vital information on a completely distinct channel. Speaking is also social in the sense that apart from what is actually being said it provides mutual assurance that the parties to it are 'playing the same game'. A superficial example of this is the speaker's pronunciation and accent, as well as what he signals by his control of various stylistic levels – all of which we have seen a bit of in historical perspective. Speaking also creates the type of social solidarity we can observe in the rapidly-changing terms of approval and disapproval affected by teen-agers: on the surface these are descriptive words showing the same grammatical behavior as 'wet', 'large' and so on, but with the significant difference that they do not really describe at all but merely express a 'personal' feeling which in fact tends to be quite rigidly applied by the entire subculture and thus serve as a valuable badge of belonging. This is merely a concentrated example of what the culture at large does with terms like 'delightful', 'silly' or 'disgraceful': these have an agreed reference, but the important difference between them and 'large', 'hot' and the like is that here, as nowhere else in the language, the speaker expresses a personal, individual involvement which is nevertheless just as much formalized by the culture as are judgements about objective size, temperature and so on. Understanding of their use (which is not at all the same thing as their dictionary meaning) in other words involves familiarity with no less a matter than the role assigned by the culture to the individual and his reactions. While this may give the impression that social acts in languages are lying about ready to be picked up and examined, they are, as is everything in a culture, part of an exceedingly complex system the study of which poses formidable difficulties but which can potentially lead to insight into some of the underlying system of the culture. This brings us up to the point where we might try to get a brief glimpse into a way in which a small fragment of such a system embedded in the standard Dutch language can give evidence of the underlying cultural agreements we have been looking for.

A language being the direct reflection of a culture, it is not at all surprising that it should turn out to give especially fine-grained expression to the institutions that are of greatest importance to that culture. One of the things that ought to interest us most about the language of the culture of the Netherlands is that whereas descriptive labels such as 'wet', 'large', 'hungry', 'hot' and so on pretty much match our English ones, it has a noticeably well-developed system of terms precisely of the 'game-playing' sort we have just talked about.

Outsiders who attempt to learn the language and adapt to the culture are apt to discover that a wide variety of situations seem to call for the expression of a judgement about their rightness or appropriateness, whereas English would often call for no such personal attitude toward the situation and in fact often provides no obvious matching word to fit it. The participants in the culture, in other words, seem to be playing by rules that call for a great deal of systematized personal reaction on the level not of communication of inherent qualities but of mutual assurance of 'belonging'. There would be little point in listing by way of demonstration all the words that belong in this realm with their 'meanings', because it is not their number or their English matchings we are talking about but their more subtle deployment as social acts. A look at just two of them in this light will go very little distance in substantiating the conclusions we will reach presently, but it will illustrate where some of the evidence lies.

Somewhat in the way that a disruption of the rules of a game can be more revealing than their smooth operation, terms of disapproval may be better indicators of what the culture expects than terms of approval. Here is a miscellaneous collection of situations in which a mild disapproval appears, signaled by X:

Here it's not as X ás in the U.S., where they even put cereal boxes on the Christmas trees – It seems rather X, all those battles where people are killed on only one side – Artists are often considered asocial people who do X things – At a celebration things are pretty X if you don't hear the word 'heartwarming' – He stood there old and tired in that X summer suit – The teacher (a child) has only one child in the class, and that child is standing in the corner; that is X.

Many of these X's can be replaced by an appropriate descriptive term in English, though few if any of them seem to add much meaning to the sentence, and in any case no one word will do for all the situations. Each of these situations is one in which a speaker or writer of Dutch used the common adjective *gek*. Though dictionaries will list the commonest meanings of this word, comparison of a large enough number of contexts like the above will show that in fact in has

167

practically no specific meaning at all. Since it can be applied to literally almost anything, it has more the nature of a label for whatever is in any way out of the ordinary or different from the expected or satisfactory – or indeed for whatever is simply unfamiliar. What falls into this category is what does not in some sense 'belong', and therefore the act of using the word *gek* does not represent the description it gives the appearance of representing but symbolizes a social agreement about what is the ordinary, expected and familiar, the standard that ideally is not deviated from. This standard may reach all the way from moral behavior to the color of one's suit, but the speakers of the language by their very uniform agreement on where the word is in place assure each other that one of the rules helping to hold society together is being observed.

This sample demonstration suggests that *gek* is a social word expressing the culture's judgement about what deviates from its tacit standards, and that the individual in using it in effect speaks on behalf of the society. There are other situations, however, in which a similar mild form of disapproval seems to be expressed on behalf of an individual:

It is X for her that she appeared on the front pages – A fashionable word, a X, worthless expression – It is naturally X when one of the volumes (of the set) is missing – I think that playing around with intellectual and social tendencies is X – She thought going arm-in-arm with another woman was X, it interfered with her walking – If you eat too little, do X things happen? – The wartime blackouts were X –

– and so is being taken for a German, being helpless with appliances that won't work, being bashful and getting an electric shock. In all these situations the word *vervelend* was used, an adjective that is very nearly as frequently used as *gek* although Dutch speakers seem to have much less consciousness of its frequency than they do in the case of *gek;* in any case it is not subjected to the ritualized denunciation that its social partner is. Here it is not easy to say what the ideal really is, the deviation from which is being disapproved of; it would have to be different in each situation. Even these few examples suggest, though, a certain social consistency in the application of the term: the individual is recognized to have a claim on a certain generalized well-being and convenience, violation of which is readily perceived by the society.

We now have two examples of social-solidarity words, one in the social realm and one in the personal, and both of them on the negative side. This takes us one short step into a complicated system in which there are numerous such terms, social and personal, negative and positive.[2] These words single out fields of judgement and its consequences in various ways and create a number of social dimensions, all of them meaningful only in their functioning as part of this system. The cultural pattern that holds all of this field together, and that is invoked and subscribed to tacitly whenever one of its members is used, is the relation between the individual and the society of which he is a part. The existence of a system of terms like the above two offers concrete evidence of an elaborate, inclusive system of abstract values and the means at society's disposal to enforce conformity to this along a wide front. It hints, further, that some cultural habits have changed rather little since the Middle Ages: it shows the individual to be thoroughly embedded in a society which sits in judgement over a wide variety of aspects of behavior, a society against the background of which the individual's self is formed by way of alertness to the opinions of others. Dutch society displays a revealing bit of self-knowledge in the well-known expression *Doe je gewoon, dan doe je al gek genoeg* — Act natural, and you're acting funny enough.

This quick glance at the way the language manifests social acts along the lines laid down by the culture suggests the continuing real existence of a uniform ethic evolved centuries ago by a self-aware but conservative middle class and given further form in the exclusive circles of a merchant elite. Even though many of the most important cultural innovators of the past came from the liberal minority, it is obvious that the real 'glue' that held the culture together and that transformed Regent culture into a viable heritage came from a class that was city-bred but that adhered to a sober and demanding bourgeois ethic that is evident in the 17th century's pictures of itself — it is written, for instance, on the faces of the five stern ladies portrayed by Frans Hals back in 1664. While the system of moral imperatives as it existed then was inevitably evolved over several centuries, it is hard to deny that its rules have generally remained remarkably stable and have cast the whole culture — Protestant, Catholic, and unchurched alike — into a mold of which no member of the culture is unaware. Probably no aspect of the culture is the object of more real or pretended disdain today than this hard-to-define system of agreements about right and wrong that shapes the individual's conception of his role. It is the confining aspects of this system that *Ik Jan Cremer* attempts to reflect in its reverse image, but it remains to be seen whether this and many similar challenges will make any serious inroads. The widespread expression of disapproval of the system almost seems like an example of the ability modern cultures have developed — very likely with each other's help — to reflect on certain of their important institutions and then insist on the periodic catharsis of a ritualistic self-criticism.

The implied ideal of the inviolability of the individual who is given security by a uniform social setting has proven to have its weaknesses, but also its strengths. The most widely-voiced criticism is that it discourages nonconformity and any impulse toward exposure of one's self, and encourages a somewhat narrow and anxious preoccupation with the behavior of others. In group interaction people tend, as we saw in Chapter 2, to be hesitant to risk exposure without the protection to their inner dignity afforded by structured situations and agreed-upon procedure, the wait-and-see attitude that has given wide currency to expressions such as *de kat uit de boom kijken* 'to see which way the cat will jump'. It is, in fact, probably not going too far to say that the development of the elegant written form of the language — itself the object of increasing ridicule — was an answer to the need for a means of expression tailored to precisely such structured situations. On the positive side, however, this ideal looks very much like the polite, sober reserve cultivated by the 17th-century merchant elite, and the high respect for the individual that inspired the culture's creative spirits from Erasmus on down. The strength of the ideal lies in the acceptance, once the inner inviolability is guaranteed, of the give-and-take that forms the viability of the culture. It is, apparently, only by creating well-secured individual bastions all playing by essentially the same rules that the clash of sharply-defined viewpoints inherent in *verzuiling* can be made productive rather than destructive.[3]

By now we have seen many times over how the continual struggles and accomodations of the past have produced today a fragmented society that hallows age-old polarizations of viewpoints in the *zuilen* that are so uniquely characteristic of the Netherlands – and, it might now be added, so uniquely suited to its conditions. A society totally split up into isolated groups could plainly not survive long, a common cultural past notwithstanding, if it had not evolved at the same time some means of ensuring consciousness in all participants of belonging to the larger whole, of 'playing the same game'. The most obvious of these means is the standard language itself, and in the last few pages we have been seeing how the language has come to formalize a well-articulated set of agreements about behavior that compensate for the tendency to find one's self-identity within the confines of the *zuil* by providing a uniform system of rules for all – including the vital rule that the beliefs of others are to be respected, that is, politely ignored except by mutual consent. But on the thoroughly practical level at which the political life on the country must be carried on, such abstract social institutions are of little use. The dozen or so political parties in existence at any one time have the function of furthering the exclusive interests of one bloc – the large ones those of the three or four *zuilen* and the small ones those of groups with more specific axes to grind. In a pluralistic atmosphere in which a broad consensus is largely lacking, some type of modus vivendi has to be found. It will be illuminating for us to consider, as a final step, how the practical level of the society's political life shows once again the operation of some of the fundamental cultural rules evolved out of the necessities of the past.

The Dutch voter casts his ballot not for personalities but for a party, the party that best represents his own particular interests. Since the interests represented by the program of one's political party tend very strongly to be bound up with many other aspects of one's life such as religious conviction, it is not at all surprising to note that the share of the total vote gained by any one party tends to be very stable and relatively predictable. The voter is presented with a list of candidates, for instance for parliament, which for each party has been made up by the small group at the top that has the actual power. Many polls and studies have shown that Dutch political life is characterized by a marked tendency to perpetuate this system: the average voter does not participate strongly in politics but is content to leave the real decision-making in the hands of these elites. Rising to a position of authority tends to be strongly admired, and a great deal of deference is shown toward the established elites. It goes without saying that there is constant criticism and resistance to the actions of those in authority, but the general benign paternalism that characterizes the whole system seems to have ways of discouraging participation at the lower levels and keeping the decision-making process firmly in the hands of those who 'know best'. Although this adds up to a certain docility on the part of the electorate, it does have the value of minimizing particularistic aggressiveness on a very fragmented political scene.

The key to the actual functioning of this political system is the rather intricate and delicately balanced procedure of give and take at the elite level that was the subject of a recent study by A. Lijphart called *The politics of accomodation.*[4] The elites, especially those of the large center parties, interact habitually in a spirit of consideration and accomodation, immediately behind which is a strong conviction that politics is not a mere game for which they can ultimately escape responsibility but a business which it is their prime responsibility to

172

keep operating. But this 'business' itself is characterized by customs and tacit agreements that make it so much like a game that Lijphart finds it natural to entitle one of his most important chapters 'The rules of the game'. The most important among these rules are the ones that call for an accepting, polite accomodation on the horizontal plane that creates a democratic atmosphere across the top, and for a mild paternalism on the vertical plane that assures the pluralized levels below that authority is in knowledgeable hands. The first of these looks so much like the accomodating spirit of the 17th-century Regents that we are almost surprised at how little some of the cultural institutions have changed over three centuries, and the second, the paternalism also characteristic of the Regents, helps to explain better the role played by the monarchy. The strongest support for the Orange monarchs comes at present from the orthodox Calvinist segment of the population, whose religious belief strongly emphasizes obedience to authority, and from the governing elites themselves who might well be expected to show loyalty to the primary symbol of their own paternalism. The entire political system is held together by what can best be called a 'Regent mentality' that is inherited from the Republic and adapted to modern conditions with overwhelming support from the society.[5]

Fortunately, though, it does not enjoy the unanimous support of the society, nor has it ever gone its way unchallenged. Of the numerous challenges that have ranged from the violent to the academic and served over the centuries to keep the Regent system acceptably sensitive to public responsibility, a few have reflected so directly the rules by which the culture operates that they can be seen, in the manner of Multatuli's *Max Havelaar,* as culture-specific myths. Let us pause one final moment to consider the nature of the most recent of these, the short-lived phenomenon that gained a certain international notoriety under the name *Provo.*

In the mid-60s a mixture of general restlessness and disaffection with society that is found among the younger generation in many countries

173

rather suddenly became focused and began moving in a .definite direction. Among the many contributing factors was no doubt the *Zo is het* affair of 1964, in which youth found itself overwhelmingly on the 'left', the side that sympathized with the shock that had been administered to the society. But the most direct cause of this focus was a series of confrontations in Amsterdam between a loose-knit group whose means of expression was the demonstration and the 'happening', and an established authority that somewhat over-zealously protected the society's deep-seated preference for the ordinary and for following fixed rules. Indignation at this treatment rapidly crystallized into an attitude that the provocation of repressive authority was a meaningful end in itself, because it forced the culture's 'Regent mentality' to display its true interest in guaranteeing the liberties only of the established elite. The prime scapegoat was the Mayor of Amsterdam, the Regent par excellence, who – like the mayors of all Dutch cities – is not elected but appointed by the Crown. By a complicated chain of circumstances that is not easy to follow thanks partly to the fact that the goals and the guiding spirits had a way constantly shifting, this general attitude of provoking authority to prove the reality of the 'Regent mentality' turned into the conscious movement known as *Provo*. In its beginning stages many of the 'happeners' were drawn from the Jan Cremer motorcycle set, but in its most creative form in 1965 the leadership bore the marks of a social level a notch or two higher. It was an urban intellectual movement restricted almost entirely to Amsterdam. This circumstance accounts for the nature of the cause célèbre that more than any other gave *Provo* what cohesive power it had and provided it with an ideal climax: in 1966 opposition to the marriage of Crown Princess Beatrix to the German Prince Claus was widespread but diffuse, until the 'Regents', in this case the cabinet, unwisely gave permission for the wedding to be held not in The Hague, the real Regent capital, but in Amsterdam, the focal point of left-wing republican feeling. *Provo* took a conspicuous part in the inevitable demonstrations preceding the wedding, and was widely held responsible for the smoke bombs that attended the royal procession and were given worldwide publicity on TV.

174

In spite of its involvement in a very sensitive political issue, *Provo* had little resemblance to a political movement but all the more resemblance to a myth. Phrases like 'the *Provo* mythology' occur with noticeable frequency in the attempts that have been made to explain the nature of the movement. Harry Mulisch, a member of the contemporary literary scene, participant in *Provo* and apparently its self-appointed historian, wrote in 1966 a somewhat tongue-in-cheek 'history' of the years 1965 and 1966 called *Bericht aan de ratten-koning*.[6] The cover leaves little room for doubt that the book is going to be about a Dutch myth, because it displays a painting. There stands, in all his fat, haughty and overdressed magnificence, the figure of Gerard Bicker, a member of a powerful family, successor to the poet Hooft as the occupant of the castle at Muiden and son of the Mayor of Amsterdam, as he was seen by the master Van der Helst around 1650 and can still be seen in the Rijksmuseum. This publication and others like it[7] make it clear that *Provo* at its best was an imaginative attempt to dramatize the contrast between an unthinking obedience to rules imposed from above and a response that gives complete rein to individual initiative. The movement was inspired by, and gave publicity to, some of the ideas of the experimental painter Constant Nieuwenhuis about the nature of the urban environment: it should, in a word, be a place where humanity's play instinct comes to the foreground. At the heart of the *Provo* mythology there was a strong element of playfulness and whimsy that constantly tended to cast the authorities in the unwelcome role of the humorless, heavy-handed oppressor. The most creative aspect of *Provo* was its publicizing of urban problems such as traffic, housing, air pollution and the attitude of the police by means of a series of 'white' plans, typical of which was the *witte fietsenplan:* automobile traffic was to be forbidden access to the center of the city with its canals and narrow streets, and instead everyone would have the use of public bicycles, to be painted white. When, amidst a great deal of fanfare, the first of these was 'presented' to the city, nobody was greatly surprised when it was immediately confiscated by the police.[8]

Not long after the royal wedding in March 1966, *Provo* lost most of its momentum and rapidly began dissolving again. During its short life it moved between serious political involvement and the most bizarre absurdities and thereby made understanding of its underlying consistency difficult. But through all this it never really lost sight of its underlying myth, which held that the culture is playing a game but needs to be reminded of this. The most logical way of forcing it to display its rules, which have a tendency to become suffocating absolutes, was to challenge it with another game: pretend to take the rules seriously while really being playful, or pretend to play while really being in deadly earnest about things. The culture's game was of course the 'Regent mentality' and the chief idea of *Provo* was simply that human life was basically play, with authority coming from within rather than from above. A younger generation abrasively renouncing the culture's proud tradition of polite tolerance and reserve that perpetuates the isolated social fortresses called *zuilen* would no doubt have gotten just as little sympathy from ancestors such as Erasmus and Coornhert as it did from its own society. But it is hard to escape a suspicion that in its brief existence *Provo* presented to the culture of the mid-60's a valuable reminder of a few of its most vital sparks.[9]

15 The horizons of the culture

A challenge like the one that has just appeared in the foreground in the previous chapter deliberately places itself at odds with 'the system', and accordingly it may be viewed either from inside this system or outside it. From the outside, it has the character of a crusade, a righteous assault on an ossified, irrelevant institution that by its very existence stands for everything that is undemocratic about society. But from the inside, such a challenge has a way of demonstrating — once the smoke has cleared, of course — that the culture operates according to rules of such pervasiveness and generality as to make it nearly impossible to create a really independent patch of ground to stand on: the challengers find themselves playing a game with recognizably similar rules. More importantly, this very difficulty of truly breaking away from traditional cultural patterns that enjoy broad acceptance would seem to imply that the continued survival of the culture depends heavily on a built-in resilience which ensures the possibility of change and therefore the support and participation of a maximum number of its members. This potentially creative response along a broad front to challenges from both within and without is merely the present-day form of a process that we have followed through well over six centuries. The well-known cultural panorama we have been observing in a very sketchy form seems eloquent enough proof that the response was indeed creative, and that in some fashion a recognizably Dutch stylization of life gave its own characteristic shape to historical events. This stylization, the 'game' played by culture that creates a meaningful context for its participants, put its

177

stamp on social history but is at its most conspicuously recognizable in the stylized manifestations given permanent form as what we have been calling myths. While it is not overly difficult — in fact, perhaps a bit too easy — to point to what seems 'characteristically Dutch' about this or that painting, drama, or social institution, accounting for what features of this cultural 'game' remain stable through centuries of change and give us our sense of one single culture is a task of a different order, one that should be undertaken a bit more diffidently.

Of the threads that run unbroken all through the colorful tapestry of cultural history, the one singled out most often is a theme that can best be called 'practicality'. The culture assigns great importance to things as they are. On the most down-to-earth level this can be discerned in a habit of businesslike pragmatism, a sober realism that assures commercial success but always skirts the edge of a preoccupation with the petty. On a more abstract level we find a visual orientation that is strikingly consistent. What could have remained a trivial and innocent delight in looking at things was raised by the professional observers of the Renaissance to the initial stages in an exact science, and by the painters of the late Middle Ages and the 17th century to a vision of vivid presence in which the most ordinary things took on a mysterious luster. Even language, which is primarily sound and only secondarily vision, is so thoroughly permeated with the cultural habit of practical observation that many of the primary literary expressions of the culture cannot be fully understood without an appreciation of their sophisticated visuality.

The businesslike pragmatism that values a practical orderliness in everyday affairs almost inevitably implies a sense for a continual process of give and take among equals, some type of interaction from which all benefit. A habit of interaction that has always been dangerously close to degenerating into a struggle for advantage at the expense of the others — one of the most frequently condemned evils of today's *verzuiling* — was somehow raised to an enlightened tolerance that developed into the set of rules by which the culture has operated

178

ever since and which has come to serve as the foundation of a complex modern society. On a higher lever this sense of the equality of individuals is the vision, captured back at the dawn of the modern era, that authority is not imposed from without but implanted within and that one finds his true self not in a rigid hierarchy but in a process of free interplay. This is the liberal ideal that in turn sowed, on the practical level, the seeds that grew into a dominant respect for individual dignity.

It is this highly formalized and ritualized give and take that more than anything else gives the culture in all periods its characteristic 'game' aspect. But an indispensable part of the definition of a game is that its participants remain at all times aware that they are playing – what any one person does makes no sense except as it follows the rules being obeyed by all.[1] The tradition of enlightened tolerance developed in the hands of the Regent class was inseparably linked to the assumption that all individuals, at all levels, are subordinate to some ultimate purpose behind the interaction in which they participate. One the one hand the 'game' itself becomes sacred in the hands of those who hold authority; the paintings produced by this culture are full of intimations of a mysterious significance attributed to the setting within which things take place, and at the culture's peak they give the world its first glimpse of a setting that is forthrightly and confidently secular. It is only a short step from here to the paternalism, the 'Regent mentality' that is one of the prime rules of the game. On the other hand, though, the setting is most assuredly a religious one: all actions are seen as subordinated to a religious purpose, and it has become a commonplace that the Dutch of this period led the way in merging Christianity and capitalism in a single ideal. The religious symbolization of this authoritarian theme came of course in the form of calvinistic Protestantism, which with its strong emphasis on the subordination of all human action to the will of God very early developed into its permanent theoretical basis. The ultimate establishment of the monarchy amounted to the creation on the secular plane of a symbolization of this subordination theme, and resulted in the 'trinity' of the well-known conservative watchword *God, Nederland en Oranje.*

By being formed around such stable themes as these — and they are intended only to be suggestive, not exhaustive — the culture is enabled to perform its primary task of providing its participants with a meaningful image of the role played by individuals in the whole. But our survey of the history of the culture up to this point seems to indicate that the individual is constantly being confronted with not one but two fundamental images that are not easy to reconcile with one another. The first of these, whose prophet is Erasmus, holds that the ultimate meaningful relation between individual and whole is one of freedom and responsibility, in other words a coordinate relation. The second is best personified by Calvin — perhaps significantly an outsider — and it proclaims the fundamental relation to be one of hierarchical ordering and constraint, in other words a subordinate relation.

At the outset of our consideration of the culture of the Netherlands the question was asked what the nature of the game was that was being played in the late 1500's and early 1600's, by common consent the crucial period in the history of the culture. Although this was asked in a somewhat rhetorical tone it did imply that the chapters to follow were going to attempt an answer, and perhaps we have now reached the point at which this should be done. If the preceding chapters have demonstrated anything clearly, it is that the stability we claimed a few lines back for the themes we found is true only in a very relative sense. The picture we get again and again is not one of stability but of a constant state of tension and change in which it is often very difficult to distinguish the dominant trends. In one form or another, the two great overarching themes of coordination and subordination always seem to be present, and in the decades just before and just after 1600 each seems to have evolved an independent strength and entered into a relation with the other that was first polarized and then belligerent. The sharp focusing of these two themes at this juncture in cultural history is epitomized by the two scholars Arminius and Gomarus, the two mythical heroes whose theological armies confronted each other on the battlefield of the Synod of Dordrecht. And yet this coincided exactly with the brief moments during which these antagonistic tendencies joined into an interplay of unprecedented harmony and fruitfulness, a blend of freedom and authority that produced the world's first genuine middle-class society in the Republic whose painters were a collective epic poet celebrating its momentous existence.

Throughout the history of the culture we find these same two themes in many different guises, in an opposition to each other that is often creative but on many occasions destructive. They provide a constantly recurring motif for the culture's most important myths such as *Sara Burgerhart* and *De boeken der kleine zielen,* and continue to reappear in more ephemeral myths such as *Provo.* They can also be plainly discerned in the constant shifting of social history, where dominant classes are repeatedly modified or replaced by those with a more creative response to the need for change. On all these various levels, the culture is simply acting out faithfully the plot that was in a certain sense preordained by its deeply rooted fundamental themes. But the real pillars of the society are not, after all, such impersonal historical forces, and even less the ingeniously constructed *zuilen,* however crucial these may be for an understanding of the history of the culture. They are participants in the culture like the thirty-six people who form the subjects of Romein's brilliant collection of essays *Erflaters van onze beschaving,*[2] those who in the most divergent ways imaginable possessed the vision to give political and artistic expression to its great underlying dialectic. In this way a culture was evolved that was enabled to break out of a narrow confinement in practical preoccupations and make its own unique contribution to Western civilization.

No aspect of this long and varied cultural development can be properly viewed apart from the physical environment that is its context.

The horizons of the culture

It is hard to deny that the narrow borders of the crowded country seem to favor a spiritual confinement, and the appreciation of its climate once composed by the poet De Genestet

O land van mest en mist, van vuilen, kouden regen,
Doorsijperd stukske grond, vol killen dauw en damp . . .*

is a theme still expressed regularly, though often less rhythmically. But if the physical environment shows few signs of changing very radically in the future, neither does the culture that has its roots there. The rules evolved over six centuries of history show a conspicuous stability, and there is little reason to think that those who play by them will not continue to find creative expressions of them at all levels. There is no reason why they should not continue to ignore the limitations of their patch of soggy ground, following an instinct put into words some seventy years ago by Henriette Roland Holst in the famous line

Holland ge biedt geen ruimte als aan den geest.†

Another sonnet belonging to the same cycle in which this line occurs captures the vision of which the culture is permanently reminded by the unimpeded views and high skies of Ruysdael, Van Goyen and Koninck:

Holland gij hebt zwellende wolken-stoeten
uit verre hemel-velden aangevlogen,
gij hebt horizonnen, zacht òmgebogen
van oost naar west zonder eenmaal te ontmoeten
lijn die ze snijdt; en wijd-gespannen bogen
van stranden en van zeeën om ze henen
gaand tot waar zij met heemlen zich verenen
die uw schijn van oneindigheid verhogen.

* O land of manure and mist, of dirty, cold rain, / Soggy little patch of ground, full of chilly dew and damp.
† Holland, you offer space for nothing but the spirit.

182

De lijnen van uw land en van uw water
wekken in ons onpeilbare gedachten
verlengen zich tot eindeloos begeren.
Onze ogen proeve' iets groots en daarvan gaat er
een trek van grootheid door ons geestes-trachten
en zijn wij thuis in grenzeloze sferen.*

* Holland you have swelling processions of clouds / drifted in from distant
celestial fields, / you have horizons, gently curved / from east to west without
ever meeting / an intersecting line; and wide-drawn bows / of beaches and of
seas round about them / going to where they unite with skies / that heighten
your appearance of unendingness. / The lines of your land and of your water /
awaken in us unfathomable thoughts / and extend on in infinite desire. / Our
eyes sense something great and from thence there moves / a trait of greatness
through the striving of our spirits / and we feel at home in limitless domains.

Notes

AN INTRODUCTORY WORD

1 The most useful general cultural history in English is J.J.M. Timmers, *A history of Dutch life and art.* London, Nelson, 1959. This is a translation of *Atlas van de Nederlandse beschaving.* Amsterdam, Elsevier, 1957. A smaller version of this but with considerably more text is *Kleine atlas van de Nederlandse beschaving.* 2nd. ed. Amsterdam, Elsevier, 1963.Cultural history is presented at a rather less austere level in the same author's profusely illustrated *Spiegel van twintig eeuwen: De mens in de Lage Landen.* Amsterdam, Elsevier, 1963. Wider in scope but with few illustrations is E. de Bock, *De Nederlanden.* 2nd ed. Hasselt, Heideland, 1963. A good brief survey but unillustrated is H.A. Enno van Gelder, *Cultuurgeschiedenis van Nederland in vogelvlucht.* Utrecht, Het Spectrum, 1965.

It is much more difficult to single out one or two general surveys of political history from the many that exist in both Dutch and English. Two that are thorough, popular, and like the last three of the above cultural histories, available in paperback editions, are Jan and Annie Romein, *De lage landen bij de zee: Geillustreerde geschiedenis van het Nederlandse volk.* 4th ed. Zeist, De Haan, 1961; and P. Geyl, *Geschiedenis van de Nederlandse stam.* Amsterdam, Wereldbibliotheek, 1961.

General and specialized works on all aspects of the history, culture, literature and language of the Netherlands are to be found listed in Walter Lagerwey's annotated *Guide to Netherlandic studies: Bibliography.* Grand Rapids, Mich., 1964.

1 THE PILLARS OF SOCIETY

1 A very useful survey of the modern society of the Netherlands is Johan Goudsblom, *Dutch society.* New York, Random House, 1967.

2 Johan Huizinga, *Homo ludens: Proeve eener bepaling van het spel-element der cultuur.* Haarlem, Tjeenk Willink, 1958. The English translation, now available in paperback, is called *Homo ludens: A study of the play-element in culture.* Boston, Beacon, 1962.

3 Huizinga, *Herfsttij der Middeleeuwen: Studie over levens- en gedachtenvormen der veertiende en vijftiende eeuw in Frankrijk en de Nederlanden.* Haarlem, Tjeenk Willink, 1952. The English version is *The waning of the Middle Ages: A study of the forms of life, thought and art in France and the Netherlands in the XIVth and XVth centuries.* New York, Doubleday, 1954.

2 SOME RULES OF THE GAME

1 *Zo is het.* Ed. J. van den Berg and others. Amsterdam, De Bezige Bij, 1964. This has come to be referred to in the Dutch press as *Pays Bah,* thanks to a pun on the French name of the country *(Pays Bas)* prominently displayed on the cover.

2 H.Daudt and B.A. Sijes, *Beeldreligie: Een kritische beschouwing naar aanleiding van reacties op de derde uitzending van Zo is het . . .* Amsterdam, Polak & Van Gennep, 1966.

3 This actress, Mies Bouwman, had gained nationwide fame a year before as the hostess in a TV marathon charity drive. The unprecedented, highly emotional success of this drive in a country where thrift and sobriety are important virtues led first to an appreciation of the persuasive power of TV itself, and later, in the *Zo is het* episode, to an alarm at its power to addict.

4 J.P. Kruijt, *Verzuiling.* Zaandijk, Heijnis, 1959. This serious sociological analysis actually begins upside down at the back of a satirical treatment of the problem called *Verzuiling: Een Nederlands probleem al of niet voorzichtig benaderd . . .;* where the serious and the playful meet in the middle stands the cartoon mentioned at the beginning of the introductory chapter, showing a number of people defiantly demonstrating for their *zuil's* card-playing club with large playing cards. The other analysis by Kruijt is 'Verzuiling in beweging? Verzuildheid in Nederland, blijvende structuur of aflopende episode? ', a chapter in *Pacificatie en de zuilen.* Meppel, Boom, 1965.

5 Goudsblom, *Dutch society,* especially the chapter entitled 'National integration'. Further literature on this phenomenon can be found in many of the footnotes to Goudsblom's chapter.

6 The development of a distinct elegant style is traced in detail in G. Brom, *Boekentaal.* Verhandelingen der Koninklijke Nederlandse Akademie van Wetenschappen, Afd. Letterkunde, N.R. 62 No. 1. Amsterdam, Noord-Holland, 1955. The standard history of the language is C.G.N. de Vooys, *Geschiedenis van de Nederlandse taal.* 5th ed. Antwerp, De Sikkel, 1952.

G.J. Renier, *The Dutch nation: An historical study.* London, Allen & Unwin, 1944, p.23.

3 THE EMERGENCE OF HOLLAND

1 See introductory chapter, note 1.

2 An English translation of this is to be found in *Reynard the Fox and other Mediaeval Netherlands secular literature.* Ed. and introd. by E. Colledge. Leiden, Sijthoff, 1967. This is one volume of a series of English translations from Dutch literature called *Bibliotheca Neerlandica: A library of Dutch classics from Holland and Belgium.*

3 English translations of *Charles and Elegast,* a portion of *Walewein* and a play called *Lancelot of Denmark* are included in the volume mentioned in note 2.

4 THE BURGUNDIAN IDEAL

1 Reproductions of this picture can be found in Timmers, *A history of Dutch life and art* as well as in *Kleine atlas der Nederlandse beschaving* (An introductory word, note 1), and in Huizinga, *Herfsttij der Middeleeuwen* (Chapter 1, note 3).

2 This portrait forms the frontispiece in Huizinga, *Herfsttij der Middeleeuwen* (Chapter 1, note 3).

5 THE BIRTH OF A NEW SYMBOLISM

1 The following sketch is based largely on the biography of Geert Grote to be found in Jan and Annie Romein, *Erflaters van onze beschaving.* 8th impression. Amsterdam, Querido, 1959. The discussion to follow of the contribution of Geert Grote ought not to leave an exaggerated impression of his originality. As an activist he built directly on the thought of many who preceded him, most important of whom was the already mentioned Johannes Ruysbroeck. Ruysbroeck was a reflective mystic who helped create a general consciousness of the unity of Lowland culture by giving voice to some of its emerging tolerant ideals and, even more, by adopting the novel device of writing – and to a great extent creating – Dutch prose.

2 The best known biography of Erasmus is probably Huizinga, *Erasmus.* Haarlem, Tjeenk Willink, 1958. This is available in English under the title *Erasmus and the age of the Reformation.* New York, Harper, 1957. An excellent biographical sketch of Erasmus is also to be found in Romein, *Erflaters van onze beschaving* (see note 1).

3 An English translation, called 'Mary of Nijmeghen', is included in *Mediaeval*

Netherlands religious literature, tr. and introd. by E. Colledge. Leiden, Sijthoff, 1967.

6 THE INGREDIENTS OF POLITICAL LIBERTY

1 Political developments in the Netherlands can be understood much better if one pauses a moment to note one or two sharply divergent developments in Spanish cultural history of the same period. During the closing decades of the 15th century, when a Spain newly united under Ferdinand and Isabella and the Netherlands found themselves under the same sovereign, different cultural traditions did not stand in the way of a modest degree of cultural diffusion; for instance the writings of the Netherlands mystics are said to have been influential in Spain. The atmosphere at the court of Charles V appears to have been cosmopolitan enough to harbor Erasmus, who in the 1520's enjoyed a popularity almost amounting to a vogue. But in the next decade much of this changed almost overnight. A harsh and intolerant climate developed that shut out thought from elsewhere and set about defending Catholicism from threats by Protestants and the Turks; by the middle of the century Erasmus was on the Index. Looked at in a somewhat wider context, this absolutism is only one aspect of a dramatic development in Spanish culture, the appearance of a new form of 'game' that took the shape of a sense of mission and an ideal of grandeur that was ultimately to find its finest expression in the Spanish Golden Age. At the period in which this uniquely Spanish cultural pattern is being established, it is hard to imagine a more alien culture than the one developing in the Netherlands: an increasing particularism contrasts with a strong centralization, a nation in the hands of middle-class merchants contrasts to one almost entirely lacking a middle class and with a great gap between rich and poor, and a marked preference for sober practicality contrasts to a dream of uniqueness and grandeur. In the years of economic troubles and widespread disillusion that came in the closing decades of the 16th century in Spain, it was this illusion of grandeur with which in 1605–14 Cervantes confronted his culture in the myth the world knows as Don Quijote. A good picture of this eventful 16th century from the Spanish point of view is J.H. Elliott, *Imperial Spain 1469-1716.* New York, St Martin's Press, 1966.

2 Nassau was a small state in central Germany around the town of Dillenburg; Orange was a tiny principality in southern France.

3 For the history of the Revolt, see especially Geyl, *The revolt of the Netherlands 1555-1609.* New York, Barnes and Noble, 1958. This is an English-language edition of part of *Geschiedenis van de Nederlandse stam* (Introductory chapter, note 1).

4 A biography of William of Orange and an assessment of his importance can be found in Romein, *Erflaters van onze beschaving* (Chapter 5, note 1).

5 These remarks on Oldenbarnevelt are indebted to the biographical sketch in Romein, *Erflaters van onze beschaving* (Chapter 5, note 1).

7 THE ANATOMY OF A GOLDEN AGE

1 Huizinga, *Nederland's beschaving in de zeventiende eeuw.* 3rd impression. Haarlem, Tjeenk Willink, 1963. The English version of this essay is in *Dutch civilisation in the seventeenth century and other essays.* London, Collins, 1968. Note also Geyl, *The Netherlands in the seventeenth century.* New York, Barnes and Noble, 1961; this is an English version of part of *Geschiedenis van de Nederlandse stam* (Introductory chapter, note 1). A lavishly illustrated recent paperback dealing with many important aspects of this period is Charles Wilson, *The Dutch Republic and the civilisation of the seventeenth century.* New York, McGraw-Hill, 1968. A study of the culture of the 17th century that was written in 1884 and has since become a classic is Cd. Busken Huet, *Het land van Rembrand: Studiën over de Noordnederlandse beschaving in de zeventiende eeuw.* The Hague, Kruseman, 1965.

2 For a discussion of Coornhert in English, see R.M. Jones, *Spiritual reformers in the 16th and 17th centuries.* Boston, Beacon, 1959.

3 A brief treatment of the various religious groups in the Netherlands is given in W. Banning, *Geestelijk samenleven in Nederland.* 3rd ed. Amsterdam, Ten Have, 1966.

4 Wilson, *The Dutch Republic* (see note 1), p. 21.

8 A MANNER OF SPEAKING

1 G.G. Kloeke 'De ondergang van het pronomen *du'*, reprinted in *Verzamelde opstellen.* Assen, Van Gorcum, 1952. *De Hollandsche expansie in de zestiende en zeventiende eeuw en haar weerspiegeling in de hedendaagsche Nederlandsche dialecten.* The Hague, Nijhoff, 1927.

2 Phonetically the modern diphthongs we are talking about are $[\epsilon i]$ and $[\text{œ} y]$, the sounds from which they developed $[\bar{\imath}]$ and $[\bar{y}]$, and an earlier stage of this latter $[\bar{u}]$. Note that this parallels closely what happened in English in about the same period: the modern diphthongs $[ai]$ in *time* and $[au]$ in *mouse* are prestige pronunciations, spread from a cultural center, that replaced the earlier $[\bar{\imath}]$ and $[\bar{u}]$ pronunciations such as we hear today in *teem* and *moose.* A further exploration of the diphthongization problem and related ones is K. Heeroma, *Hollandse dialektstudies: Bijdrage tot de ontwikkelingsgeschiedenis van het algemeen beschaafd Nederlands.* Groningen, Wolters, 1935.

3 For further details see De Vooys, *Geschiedenis van de Nederlandse taal* (Chapter 2, note 6).

4 W. Hellinga, *De opbouw van de algemeen beschaafde uitspraak van het Nederlands.* A dissertation published in 1938, this is now available in *Bijdragen tot de geschiedenis van de Nederlandse taalcultuur.* Arnhem, Gysbers & Van Loon, 1968.

5 This has recently been republished as Petrus Montanus, *De spreeckonst.* Ed. W.J.H. Caron. Groningen, Wolters, 1964.

9 A MYTHOLOGY OF THE VISUAL

1 Recalling the discussion of the *Rederijkers* in Chapter 5, it is surely not accidental that the new Regent culture develops such strikingly game-like forms not in a city like Leiden with its cosmopolitan, Humanistic scholarly atmosphere created by renowned figures such as Scaliger and Stevin, but in Amsterdam, the city most heavily indebted to the strongly Medieval *Rederijkerskamers* with their scientific-didactic-cultural mission. At the beginning of the 17th century Amsterdam was the home of two thriving Chambers, one of them recently transplanted from the South. Their activities led ultimately to the founding of the *Schouwburg,* Amsterdam's first formal professional stage, in 1637, for the opening of which Vondel wrote his classic *Gijsbrecht van Aemstel,* to be discussed below.

2 It is worth noting in passing that this very same conviction, transferred to the theological level, formed the basis two centuries later of opposition to the French Revolution's ideal of popular sovereignty and has become the central tenet of today's right-wing Anti-Revolutionary Party.

3 Timmers, *Kleine atlas van de Nederlandse beschaving,* p. 139.

4 Good reproductions of all the paintings about to be discussed are to be found in the illustrated cultural histories listed in footnote 1 of the introductory chapter. The greatest disadvantage is that they are all in black and white, which will require a certain amount of imagination in reading the discussion to follow. Readers who prefer to form their own opinions about what they see will want to get some full-color reproductions of works of the three painters in question from a library. The extra trouble involved will be more than compensated for by any new trains of thought about the cultural significance of painting that grow out of leafing through some of the handsome volumes now in print.

5 It is hard to resist mentioning here a minor work of a few years ago that illustrates in an amusing way the apparent inexhaustibility of this culture's favorite mythical expression. Godfried Bomans' *Erik, of het klein insectenboek* is an allegory on modern social life which has a little boy visit the world of the insects – who turn out to be all too human in their ways. The

189

interesting aspect of this charming story is Bomans' device for bridging the gap between reality and the dream world where the shift from human to insect gives us a detached viewpoint and shows with its crazy logic the absurdity of the rules of behavior: Erik departs from his familiar setting and dreams his way into its mythical model by climbing into . . . a painting.

10 LITERARY REFLECTIONS

1 It might be mentioned, however, that our more or less arbitrarily chosen base-points anchored in literary works correspond rather well to a periodization in social history pointed out by Romein in the preface to *De lage landen bij de zee* (Introductory chapter, note 1). *Van den vos Reinaerde* falls exactly halfway between feudalism's peak at about 1100 and its final collapse around 1400; *Mariken van Nieumeghen* heralds the dominance of the Regent class in the middle of the 16th century; Hooft's drama of 1613 celebrates the climax of Regent culture, and Jan Luyken's poems coincide with its first long step toward decline – a stage not singled out by Romein. Continuing with Romein's periods: in 1747 the Bourgeoisie appears on the stage, and Van Effen's *Hollandsche Spectator* appeared 1731-35; in 1795 this class took power temporarily, and *Sara Burgerhart* (Chapter 11) appeared in 1785; in 1848 it took power firmly, and *Camera Obscura* (Chapter 12) appeared in 1845; in 1898, finally, the Bourgeoisie had to share its privileged position with less fortunate social levels, and *De boeken der kleine zielen* (Chapter 13) appeared in 1902.

2 Poetic expression as essentially the verbal elaboration of a picture is, to be sure, neither specifically Dutch nor unique to Luyken's time. Two of the best-known works in the literature of the Netherlands, Roemer Visscher's *Sinne-poppen* and Cats' *Sinne-beelden,* both written a half century before Luyken, are collections of instructive poems commenting on series of engravings.

11 NOONTIME: SARA BURGERHART

1 The title 'Prince of Orange' now no longer implied any real governing authority in the principality of Orange itself, since it had been incorporated into France in 1713 by the Treaty of Utrecht. But today the names of both Nassau and Orange are still part of the formal title of the reigning monarch: *Koning(in) der Nederlanden, Prins(es) van Oranje-Nassau,. . .*

12 MID-AFTERNOON: CAMERA OBSCURA

1 Romein, *De lage landen bij de zee,* vol. 3, Ch. 3.
2 The birthday is not, as for instance in the U.S., one's exclusive personal property but rather belongs to one's family and closest friends. It is quite in order to congratulate someone for his wife's birthday, and the person celebrating is normally expected to be available to entertain family and friends who need no invitation. Saint Nicholas, who happens to be the patron saint of Amsterdam, celebrates his birthday by giving little gifts which mysteriously show up, accompanied by rhymes, in each family circle.

13 EVENING: SMALL SOULS

1 The English version is *Small Souls.* New York, Dodd Mead, 1932.
2 'Multatuli' was the pseudonym of Eduard Douwes Dekker, and *Max Havelaar* tells the story of an idealistic and courageous civil servant who accepts an administrative position in the East Indies but is soon forced to resign in frustration, shock and disgrace when he refuses to accept his government's brutal exploitation of its empire. This outwardly simple story is told in a counterpoint with another story which serves as its frame and which is set back home in the narrow bourgeois world that complacently and smugly gives its assent to the colonial brutality being experienced at first hand by Max Havelaar. In the last few pages Multatuli brings his whole elaborately developed game tumbling down by making his characters evaporate before our eyes and stepping forward in his own person with an appeal to the conscience of King and people. The most recent English version is *Max Havelaar or the coffee auctions of the Dutch Trading Company.* Tr. Roy Edwards, introd. D. H. Lawrence. Leiden, Sijthoff, 1967.

14 CONTEMPORARY CHALLENGES

1 *Ik Jan Cremer.* Amsterdam, De Bezige Bij, 1964. Published in English as *I Jan Cremer.* Introd. by Seymour Krim. New York, Shorecrest, 1965.
2 Some other words belonging to this same social system are *raar* 'funny, strange', *vies* 'outwardly disgusting', *naar* 'leaving an unpleasant effect'; *fatsoenlijk* 'following the accepted standard of decency', *keurig* 'following the accepted standard of order and neatness', *leuk* 'leaving a pleasant – or, ironically, unpleasant – feeling'; all of these are in daily use by everyone, with relatively little specific content.
3 A word that directly reflects this cultural pattern, and hence has no exact match in English, is *brutaal.* This is a descriptive term, again a negative one, analogous to the systematic terms discussed above, but with the difference that

it refers only to persons. Put in the simplest terms, *brutaal* describes the person who does not observe the culture's requirement concerning polite reserve. Since this extends to superiors and equals alike, the word is not well translated by 'insolent', which applies only to a stepping out of bounds with relation to a superior. One who is *brutaal* ignores the personal restraint rule and asserts himself, and instead of scrupulously respecting others he invades their right to an unchallenged personal stronghold — a personality type carried to its logical extreme in the character of Jan Cremer.

4 Arend Lijphart, *The politics of accomodation: Pluralism and democracy in the Netherlands.* Berkeley and Los Angeles, University of California Press, 1968. A witty, highly individual analysis of the current political scene in the Netherlands is Henry Faas, *God, Nederland en de franje: Necrologie van het Nederlandse partijwezen.* Utrecht, Bruna, 1967.

5 A good example of the sensitivity of the present-day Regents to the precariousness of the game in a pluralistic society is that in spite of widespread cries for measures against the Socialist TV corporation, the responsible ministry declined to react officially to the *Zo is het* offense because of the clear danger of sharpening differences between *zuilen*.

6 Harry Mulisch, *Bericht aan de rattenkoning.* Amsterdam, De Bezige Bij, (Sept.) 1966.

7 For instance *Provo: Kanttekeningen bij een deelverschijnsel.* Ed. F.E. Frenkel. Amsterdam, Polak & Van Gennep, (Nov.) 1966.

8 The other 'white' plans were the *witte huizenplan* offering a solution to the housing problem, the *witte schoorstenenplan* suggesting a way to clean the air, and the *witte kippenplan* proposing that an unarmed, genial police force play an entirely unaccustomed role — *kip* 'chicken' is an Amsterdam slang word for 'policeman'.

9 It is worth mentioning as a cultural footnote that this whole facet of culture focused on by *Provo* is coming to be referred to increasingly frequently by the word *ludiek,* apparently popularized by Huizinga. Where *speels* means 'playful' in more or less the same sense as the English word, *ludiek* refers specifically to the permanent, built-in play element in culture.

15 THE HORIZONS OF THE CULTURE

1 We have had repeated occasions for noting that one of the purest examples of a formalized set of rules followed by all participants is the language they use. For the mythmakers of the culture from Erasmus through Hooft to Wolff and Deken, Beets and Couperus, in a peculiarly direct way the style is the person. The emergence of the Southern 'elegant' style was turned by the culture into a highly formalized means of presenting an image of personal politeness and

polish, and by the present day this alternative use of two stylistic extremes with many shadings in between has developed into a sophisticated game, the exact rules of which have yet to be studied. The typical *vergadering* context mentioned in Chapter 2 is the arena in which this game is perhaps at its most stylized. In this situation formal and informal language stand in a somewhat polarized relationship to each other, and experienced speakers develop a very delicate feeling for the timing and effect of components taken from one level to the other. This manipulation of complex stylistic rules also illustrates the idea that participants in a game must always remain aware that they are playing: An ironic use of elegant style as a device for a refined self-mockery is a very characteristic form of Dutch humor, and the elegant style's inherent leaning toward the pompous and the absurd is exploited by many humorists. One of the more successful of these is the popular writer Simon Carmiggelt, who in his short daily columns in an Amsterdam paper cultivates a style that is a blend of man-in-the-street speech and exquisitely timed solemnities.

2 See Chapter 5, note 1.